Becoming You

C. W. Brister

BROADMAN PRESS
Nashville, Tennessee

To Mark and Rhonda

"Heirs together of the grace of life"

4253-32
ISBN: 0-8054-5332-6

Library of Congress Catalog Card Number: 79-57361
Dewey Decimal Classification: 155.5
Subject heading: YOUTH//ADOLESCENCE
Printed in the United States of America

Contents

Preface

Becoming You is a special invitation to shape your own unique future. The front line with the title reads: "a young person's guide for living." This book provides a spark to strike fire with your enthusiasm and imagination rather than offering a grand design for living. True, your future begins with a plan. You already have the basic raw materials for existence. My offer here is to assist you in charting the course your life should take and to alert you to some dangers and resources along the way. You need to feel free to grow. Then, the life you build with the help of God, parents, teachers, and friends will be your very own.

This book is constructed on the foundation of my earlier work: *It's Tough Growing Up.* We cannot roll back the clock. America has undergone some profound changes since that work was published. Youth today are a colorful mix of the Protestant work ethic and flower children, of involved protesters and laid-back postponers, aggressive go-getters and passive resisters to change. With so much talk about the Me generation—people whose interests extend as far as the mirror—we sometimes forget that a new world is being born. You will find fresh ways of expressing the philosophy that made *It's Tough Growing Up* worthwhile to earlier readers.

My purpose is to help extend your vision past the mirror to all the worlds of your living. You will detect central themes like: celebrating youth's passion for life, discovering personal identity and goals, and surviving in a brutal culture. Well-informed students of personality tell us how valuable daydreaming may be for creative use of the imagination. Chapter 1 plugs into the pleasant visions of an imaginary young man. Unfolding chapters address issues like: becoming your own person, managing sexuality, discovering a purpose, and making decisions in an enlightened, responsible way. *Becoming You* is packed with evidence and insights that will help when things get you down and move you toward maturity.

As a young person, making it—expecting the best and surviving the worst—is your present life's work. Growing up can be scary and crazy and fun. Sometimes it's tough and brutal; at other times tender and beautiful. Adolescence is like a prolonged high wire act without a safety net always being there. You can't be spared life's sorrows if you want its sparkles, too.

Notice, you are being addressed in an informal, personal manner. I am making a pitch for full personhood for you, us (middle-aged adults), and them (all "the others" in mankind's larger fellowship). In fact, this is your invitation to dialogue so that you will not feel alone in your life search. Most grown-ups believe in you, though we often communicate on different wave lengths.

What—beyond physical attractiveness, intelligence, group acceptance, music, modern styles, and intimacy—does youth value? Money? Yes, young people pump more than twenty billion dollars into the U.S. economy each year. Automobiles and motorcycles? Yes, with a set of wheels one is suddenly free from parental restraints, linked mystically with the throbbing engine's power. Sports? Travel? Dating? Protest? Sex? Freedom? Yes, all these things and more. Shifting from longtime goals, characteristic of maturity, the young person wants more and more *now*. His immediate goals are: (1) early attainment of full adult status (including sexual gratification), and (2) economic independence from parents and powerful providers.

He wants to be on his own today. Such goals place a heavy burden on you and your parents.

Many contemporary young persons are decidedly religious, yet they reject as hypocritical any church that fails to meet human needs. Be forewarned! Extremists are everywhere. The number of far-out cults and para-church groups has vastly multiplied and their influence has become global. Idealistic young people are vulnerable to unconventional movements like Sun Myung Moon's Unification Church, Hare Krishna's Hindu consciousness, and Scientology's mind control. Simplistic systems of certain religious leaders offer instant answers but close the spirit to personal growth in a powerful way. Now is the time for nurturing one's faith and inner life through authentic religious experience. For such reasons we shall explore certain aspects of growing up in light of Christian truth.

The book is addressed to students, parents, and teachers in church and public schools. Guidance counselors aiding adolescents, who wish to make sense out of life and something of themselves in society, will find wisdom here for their work. Presentation of these ideas presupposes small group discussions by healthy, growing young people.

Fittingly, examples and case studies of teenagers are provided as models. The names, locations, and circumstances of persons mentioned in cases have all been changed. Conversations are essentially what people said, rather than their actual words. They mirror the challenges coming your way. Just write in your name with the title: ______________________ ______________—*Becoming You.* This book recognizes that you are special.

Writing is always a shared venture. Suggestions from gifted workers with youth: Cindy Bryant, Nancy Ellett, Lisa Gardner, and Joe Palmer; and talented young people: Becky and Beryl Bradshaw, and Sherry and Karen Fowler have strengthened this book. I wish to thank also Mark and Rhonda Brister, my son and his wife, for inspiration and editorial assistance. My wife, Gloria, sparked my best effort and consulted wisely and encouragingly during the book's preparation. Thanks also to hundreds of young people who, in family-life conferences, have raised questions about things that matter. Their enthusiasm for life promises to each of us a future full of hope.

1
Dream, Dream, Dream

One man with a dream, at pleasure,
  Shall go forth and conquer a crown;
And three with a new song's measure
  Can trample an empire down. . . .
For each age is a dream that is dying,
  Or one that is coming to birth.

(Arthur O'Shaughnessy, 1844-1881, "Ode")

This book is about a dream. It is not a fantasy, a utopian vision, or a hallucination. There is a great difference between a delusion and a dream. The former has no basis in fact. It is an unfounded, mistaken impression of reality. An illusion may be induced by drugs, such as LSD, or produced by an unhealthy emotional state. Whereas, *dream,* as used here, implies a view of life marked by order, power, mystery, comradeship, hope, and joy. It is a personal dream, but one shared by many others.

You are a central figure in the drama. It is early morning. A lonely jogger—a young person in a hurry—strides along a street in a suburban neighborhood. He is outfitted in blue shorts, a white T-shirt, and blue jogging shoes. Sounds of morning, the voices of birds claiming their territory and trucks thundering along a nearby freeway, break the silence. An elderly couple, he quite pouched and she slightly stooped, shuffle along hand in hand. Their conversation is barely audible as the runner chugs by, now short of breath. A fifteen-minute-mile walker, a person of middle age no longer struggling with stopwatch time, moves briskly toward home, his shower, breakfast, and working day.

Replaying the scene in slow motion, we see that Jim White, the lonely jogger dressed in blue, is Everyman. He is *you*! Jim is a symbolizer—representing all youth—those who are moving from the person one is now to the "person not yet." Paradoxically, he is both a growing individual and still being born. We sense that God has not finished with him yet. The middle-aged walker represents Jim's father, a mentor and model, who is further along life's journey than Jim. He's a funny guy in some ways; "different" may be a better word for it. Yet, he and Jim's mother have been so helpful in assisting Jim to make it. We recognize the aging couple as grandparent figures—Jim's and those of millions of other American youth—who have little time left. They appear at peace with life, slightly over-the-hill, yet grand to be with on special occasions and holidays. At this stage, they need Jim's love and support more than Jim needs their care.

Family members like Jim's form your own cheering section along the jogging tracks of life. Other persons join your support group—peers who have come to be special in classes, extracurricular activities (life sports), church choir, during fun times, or at work. Your teachers at school and church believe in you and want the best for you. They take pardonable pride in each of your achievements and grieve when you are troubled. One's family and friends expect the best, not as a put-down when one fails, but as a positive attitude on all that one does.

Jogger Jim is a dreamer on a journey toward wholeness. He daydreams while running. He feels lonely but recognizes that there are many other runners, too. For discussion purposes, let's follow our young seeker for wisdom through a series of reveries. We shall join him, as the first dream unfolds, at one of several parties.

A Non-Birthday Party

Jim White moved to the Midwest when he was fifteen. His father got a new job—large salary increase with a promotion—and moved Jim, his mother, brother, and sister hundreds of miles from their home. Breaking into the school cliques that flocked together—athletes, outstanding students, and people with special interests—was tough. Jim found the group in tenth grade too large to form lasting friendships. The cliques were too small or exclusive for easy attachment.

Since Jim's greatest pleasure in life was running, he tried out for the track team. The guys had their own specialties. Only one or two of them recognized his need for new friends. Most grown-ups sense the value of personal friendships and group activities in one's identity formation. It's hard for one's peers to sense the loneliness of feeling like an outsider when people are all around.

At the same time Jim's dad moved up in job status, his work load got heavier. There were night meetings and out of town trips. He supervised an office staff and monitored field production. As a result there were fewer times for the family to be together. Jim's attachments with adults were breaking off before new ties were formed with peers. There seemed to be no substitutes for the parental guidance he was losing and family safety he was giving up.

Taking driver's education helped Jim to adjust to these unprecedented social changes. He had to keep pace with a fast moving academic schedule. In the new high school, teaching modules shifted every twenty minutes—two or three a period. The atmosphere on his open campus was like a university. Few people seemed to care who he was or where he was headed. Being behind the wheel of a specially equipped automobile, with the safety an instructor provided, was great.

When Jim's sixteenth birthday rolled around, it was one of the most exciting and depressing times of his life. He got his driver's license that day. Only one thing was "bad news"—nobody noticed! His classmates were so preoccupied with surviving their own over-organized lives that there was no birthday party. Kids in the big city school seemed to care less about each other than his old friends back home. They worried about grades, dates, money, college admissions, and jobs, but not about each other. In fact, Jim's self-esteem bombed out even though he had that magic new driver's license. That's when he fantasized a birthday party.

Jim pretended that two buddies on the track team, Kim and Charlie, discovered it was his birthday. They had fun eating pizza one night, teasing him good-naturedly about Janna (a cute blond), then going for a ride in Kim's pickup truck. Everyone else forgot or didn't know Jim was sixteen. Still, Kim's and Charlie's friendship put the stars back into his sky. Without his new friends, life would have been depressing indeed. If it only had been more than make-believe!

Thus far, we have imagined a young jogger searching for his own identity through certain changes adolescence brings. That Jim is a runner recognizes new growth—physiological and chemical changes that have been occurring over the years. That he is a member of a family in a mobile society reminds us of group affiliations, geographical changes, and new social settings. Scene 1—the non-birthday party—reminds us that things do not always go perfectly at sixteen. One must make it in a high-speed, secular environment where fewer people seem to care.

Becoming James Warren White, with an identity of one's own, is a lifelong process. Yet, one's adolescent years are crucial for identity formation. It is a time of inward searching, insecurity, false starts, self-doubt, and struggle with one's environment. Defining one's self and establishing one's place in society are major hurdles toward a productive life. If resolution of one's identity fails and a developmental crisis persists, a person may end in a state of role confusion, isolation, and interpersonal conflict.[1]

The Garden Party

The reverie persists as the scene shifts. Jim White imagines that he is twenty-two, has worked each summer, and gone to university four years. A liberal arts major, he is interested in journalism, writing, perhaps studying abroad on a scholarship. He and Nancy Cates will be married the end of June, following graduation. Their parents have pooled resources and are sending them to Europe for a honeymoon trip. They hope to get as far as Zagreb, Yugoslavia, a large city behind the Iron Curtain, and down the coast to one of the world's prettiest beaches.

In the dream, Jim and his bride-to-be are honorees at a garden party. Their host and hostess are prized faculty friends, the Votmanns of the English department. Ted Votmann was Jim's favorite professor. A mixed group of graduating seniors and business and professional people from their church were there. Nancy and Jim noticed how some guests stuck to themselves after they had gone through the serving line; others were outgoing and friendly. Dick Nash, an electrical engineer, particularly intrigued Jim. He was part of a design group for the sophisticated F-16 fighter bomber—a futuristic aircraft on order by the United States Air Force and several European governments.

Nash explained to his sensitive young friend, Jim, that the plane provided no surface contacts between the "stick"—traditionally moved by pilots for vertical and horizontal responses—and the ailerons, flaps, and so on. The multimillion dollar airplane, propelled by high-velocity jet power, is a computerized data bank of electronic impulses, sensors, decoders, and programmed responses.

"In a Piper Cub," Nash noted, "the pilot moved a stick that was tied by small cables to the ailerons (flaps). In this plane, the *feel* of the stick is still there but it is tied only to sensitive computers. Pulling slightly to the left, with ten or fifteen pounds pressure, would have the ship three hundred degrees into a roll at unbelievable speed."

While Jim was like a fish out of water with jargon like thrust reverser, sound suppressor, engine pod, and pylon, he was jolted with a new realization. As he and Nancy moved into the future, Jim was certain that different types of specialists—workers with words like himself, surgeons, accountants, teachers, social workers, and systems engineers—would be thrown together in a new cultural situation. William Irwin Thompson has called this synthesis a new renaissance in which "mystics" and "systems engineers" must learn to live together, learn from one another, and contribute to life.[2] Mystics are inner-oriented persons, accepting and trusting of feelings and intuition. They are not accustomed to taking life apart or looking objectively at scientific data like an engineer. Both mystics and engineers, however, are mutually dependent upon international political agreements, oil cartels, and shrewd financiers to make their new renaissance world work.

The garden party dream was a new segment of Jim White's development. He got a vision of the significance of vocational choice as the maximal use of one's God-given talents for useful purposes. He foresaw an humbling interdependence of people and nations in order to help life function in the future. How big were the choices that shaped his destiny! Where will we be in the twenty-first century? he wondered.

The Tenth Anniversary Party

When one is dreaming, his fancies can push ahead in time. Jim White had wondered about his identity and envisioned his marriage and vocation. He had few details in mind, yet he knew that life would be richer with someone like Nancy Cates to share it. Still, our young jogger wondered about his destiny. Where, ultimately, was he headed? What should his values be? Would faith in God and fidelity to Jesus Christ as Lord of life make a difference? With such issues in mind, the dream of a tenth anniversary reunion for his high school senior class began.

More than one hundred people gathered in a great hall appeared in Jim's dream. It was a country club ballroom, decorated with colorful banners of Colonial High School (his alma mater). He had served on the planning committee, chaired by Sherry Goldstein. His former associates at Colonial had scattered across America and the world. The people in his dream were drawn by a desire to renew ties with former classmates, meet their spouses (though several were still single), compare life achievements, and talk about the future.

Rick and Wanda Baker had flown in from Juneau, Alaska, where he was involved in politics and she in journalism. Mack Borne, a first mate on a tanker operated by an oil company, and his wife, Judy, had established themselves in Baltimore. She was an attorney. They had a unique sense of fidelity, since he was gone about six months each year. Margaret Horne, a single schoolteacher, had lost weight. She looked better than Jim had remembered her at Colonial High and talked of curriculum tracks, foreign travel, and educating America's young.

Ninety-five percent of the persons in the ballroom held cocktail glasses. The tiny bell-shaped containers sparkled under the spinning chandeliers. Champagne seemed to lubricate conversation and ease social reentry after a decade apart. Since he and Nancy did not drink alcoholic beverages, Jim felt different but not uneasy. There were dainty edibles from the hors d'oeuvre trays. Disco music filled the air. Dancers swirled and touched in the semi-darkness. Sherry Goldstein basked in all her glory.

It was a good suggestion to have this tenth anniversary reunion, thought Jim. Informal conversations closed the gap with high school friends he had admired a decade before. Their faces were already etched by time, aged by divorce (in numerous instances), matured by family responsibilities, and tired by schedules of work and play. The daydream projected Jim into full adulthood. He saw how fatigue could become a constant companion. He sensed that many adults live too close to frustration, anger, and depression—that zest, love, and laughter could be in short supply.

Daydream As Clue to One's Future

Jim recovered from his reverie. How long have I been daydreaming? he wondered, after being lost in thought. Have I had three dreams or a long dream with three scenes?

Earlier, our jogger, Jim White, was described as a dreamer on a journey toward wholeness. He wanted to discover himself, God's purpose for his life, something about his mate, and his destiny. Jim appreciated the daydreams as a clue to his future. He was no Superman but he was for real. And that girl, Nancy Jean Cates, was real and beautiful, too. To make sense of his dreams, Jim decided to share them privately with a friend, Clyde Dodson, his youth minister.

"What did the dreams mean?" he asked Clyde. "There must be some reason for them." They dialogued about the symbolism and substance of the three parties. Healthy responses came as Jim answered his own question.

"The non-birthday party revolved around my own identity, fear of moving from familiar people and surroundings, and struggle to become my own man," observed Jim.

"That's quite an order for most of us," Clyde responded. "Normally, we are clarifying basic issues like identity all along in life. Great insight, Jim!"

"The garden party addressed issues like relating to the opposite sex, marriage," reflected Jim, "and my sense of vocation." (Pause.) "Clyde, I see myself as the mystic at Professor Votmann's that night. I have to push hard to get excited about fields like economics and engineering. The engineer, Dick Nash, helped me to clarify some things about my life's work."

"Do you think that what you do with your life matters in God's eyes?" inquired Clyde, drawing out his friend.

"Certainly!" came Jim's reply. "God's persons should have a sense of destiny, of purpose, and the will to achieve it. I often ask myself, 'Will Christ as Lord of my life make a difference?' "

"Identity and vocation," responded Clyde, "are two of life's central issues. You're thinking about them, Jim. That's great! You mentioned 'a sense of destiny.' Does destiny tie in with the tenth anniversary party?"

"I'm not sure about the future," Jim sighed. "That's heavy! I'm so wrapped up in my own game and getting it together now that I really have no idea what lies ahead."(Pause.) "At least I know some things I don't want to happen. I don't want a marriage separated by time and space, like Mack and Judy Borne, and I don't want to depend on alcohol to help me through trying times." His voice trailed off into silence.

"Listen Jim, I have to run now," Clyde said. "Good to talk with a real dreamer. Don't sweat the small stuff!" Clyde grinned and was gone. There the dream ended. Or did it? Perhaps it had only begun. Thank goodness Clyde didn't use the occasion to preach to me, thought Jim. He knew one thing for sure: it's tough growing up.

As you can see, this book is something of a treasure map to help you find your own way. I want to share some of the road with you and can provide a few clues. Ultimately, the treasure you discover will be your own.

2
Stranded in the Present

If a man does not keep pace with his companions perhaps it is because he hears a different drummer. Let him step to the music which he hears, however measured or far away.

(Thoreau: *Walden*)

You are one of nearly thirty million teenagers in the United States. Like other young people, you enjoy fun and games, athletic contests and winning, music with a favorite beat, money and clothes, cars and dates, travel and movies. Who wants to get "aced out" of his chance at life?

The ordeal of being young isn't child's play, however, It's a time of seeking to find who one is and searching for a place in life. Since each person matures at his own pace, your big problem just now is yours uniquely. Jane may feel self-conscious. She wonders: How can I get over my shyness and become more outgoing? Kevin may resent being lumped into the teenage mode. He thinks: Teenagers aren't all bad. Most of us are just trying to live day by day in a confused and mixed-up world. And Debbie may know a boy she's dying to date. Her big question today is: How am I going to get inside that lonely guy and make him ask me for a date?

Some midteeners have an overweight problem, some are very poor, many are ashamed of their parents. Some fear they won't amount to much. Others wonder jealously why some lucky people have all the fun. You may feel too tall, pimply, fat, black, perplexed, poor, handicapped, or different to mix. But in one major respect you're like every other adolescent: you're stranded in the present.

You're not impressed with adult talk of World War II, the Great Depression, or the big swing sound of popular music in the forties. The past has had it. It seems unreal and certainly old-fashioned. Neither are you worried about where you'll live when you retire or if you anticipate a space trip to Mars in 2001. True, a majority of today's graduates will be entering jobs that did not exist when they were born. But things are so unpredictable that "tomorrow" seems irrelevant in your life. As with Jim White, thinking in the future tense is reserved for daydreams and fantasies.

What is left, of course, is the present. Today becomes the one rock of constancy in a shifting sea of change. With a slightly unreal past and an uncertain future, an intensification of today results. Admit it. You're face to face with life.

Face to Face with Life

Maybe Shakespeare was right. All the world's a stage. You are one of the players. The audience—parents, teachers, relatives, your friends—prepares to applaud your performance. A voice within, like a director backstage, says: "Once in a lifetime my destiny calls me. I'm gonna do great things." You shake inside wondering, Is this my moment? There are doubts, What if I blow it? and feelings of high resolve, But they're depending on me. I can't let them down!

You are pressed by today's demands and tomorrow's uncertainties to live for the moment. Certain advantages of living in the present are obvious. You can travel light and be ready for anything. You are more flexible and superficially, at least, more comfortable. You owe nobody anything. You can select people as models who are real in your life now and imitate their admired qualities—clothes, hair styles, ideas, values. Problems of "cutting the apron strings" from home abound, but parents mean less and peers mean more as you grow older.

Above all, you can live today. A nineteen-year-old student, injured fatally in an automobile accident, said just before he died: "Don't cheat me God. I want to live!" You understand what he was trying to say and feel pity that he did not survive.

But more, there is a strong sense that you must get maximum mileage in the present. You want to live, too.

There is another side to this out-of-dateness with the past and future, however, with this increasing emphasis on the lived moment. For one thing, your self-identity is shaped in large measure from family relationships and experiences. By the time you're in senior high school a set, or life-style, has developed. If you fail to learn the meaning of maleness and femaleness, work, play, adulthood, and social membership from your mother and father, where do you discover how to be human?

Two, you need varied models with whom to identify. This is why friends—young and older—are crucially important. You must filter or winnow what is valuable, enduring, and worth keeping from significant others. Being selective, partial, and cautious in who you wish to be like is not easy.

You reflect the nonhero figures, film themes, and music of today, as well as the scapegoating tactics of cynical people. Who are you like or unlike in your tastes? By such a selective process you gain an ego identity—you become a real person.

Again, some teenagers, like Biff in Arthur Miller's *The Death of a Salesman*, appear unable to "take hold of life." You may know someone with so many anxieties that he doesn't know who he is or where he is going. Feelings of unrelatedness, of being adrift, of not being able to hold on to anything may be normal if they are temporary. Some of your acquaintances may appear "out of it" with drug problems, antisocial views, and ideas that sound emotionally sick. They are hurting badly.

There is danger, too, in contemporary hedonism. The philosophy of finding pleasure in disconnected moments was expressed by a rock group leader thus: "Never have a steady job. Keep crazy hours. Get stoned. Play music. Draw constant attention, and make lots of money." Would you agree?

Jean-Paul Sartre, the French existentialist, once described

the human condition of sin as life "empty of God" and lived "in bad Faith" (that is, with falsehood) toward oneself and others.[3] The biblical idea of sin means essentially that one mismanages his or her life. To the degree that you discover God's purpose—your reason for living—and follow it, the happier you'll be.

I like to see young people lead responsible and satisfying lives. Success, however modest or marginal, is always more convenient and enjoyable than defeat. A search for identity can be an uncomfortable experience for students, who list anxiety and depression as persistent maladies. One way of coping with new and unfamiliar stresses is to educate oneself in what life's all about.

What's It All About?

One teenager said: "Right now, I don't want to do anything like study or anything that takes real concentration except just thinking about problems, dreaming, and things of this nature. Consequently, I don't do things that I should do. I don't even try." Your problems seem private and personal—at times unanswerable.

It takes time to realize that personal doubts and anxieties are universal. To ask existential (life and death) questions is to be more human than otherwise. What pains you hurts all other teenagers, too, though you must solve problems for yourself.

"I realize," said Jimmy, "that there are a lot of things I don't understand. I'll just have to experience them myself and suffer the consequences." You certainly would not like it if your parents took all the risks for you, all the bumps, self-doubts, and joys of discovery. You want to be free to grow, to see for yourself what it's all about.

It's About Self-Discovery. Grown-ups think teenagers wear funny clothes, enjoy odd diets, and say and do strange things. There are big battles occasionally over minor matters like Bill wearing a ragged sweat shirt and paint-stained jeans, rather than a clean shirt and pressed Levis to school; or LeaAnn wearing a slogan T-shirt and shorts, rather than a dress to a party.

Kids talk about their battles for independence from the older generation. Their questions are really protests.

Why do parents force us to do things against our will?

Parents say they understand, but do they really?

Why don't parents let us do a little more on our own, like selecting clothes or deciding where to go on a date?

Our parents tell us to act our age, but why don't they treat us our age?

You may appreciate seventeen-year-old Barbara's discontent:

> Every day I ask myself why I am not the person I would like to be. My relationship with myself is a very unhappy one. I am temperamental, a person of many moods. I pretend, so people cannot discern it. This is what I hate most about my life. I always act not like my true self.
>
> Fundamentally, I am a friendly person. But my teachers think that I am cold. I hate all of them so much that I just want to say, "(I reject) you superior egotistical people. I am as good as you." When I am with people who have confidence in me, I do good work. With those who treat me as an accessory to a machine, I become stupid. All I really want of life is to have someone who can accept me as I am.[4]

If you feel complex, angry, moody—like Barbara—don't be surprised. You're trying to figure out a lot of mysteries and to handle changes in growing up—tasks like: (1) managing sexual feelings, thoughts, dreams, fantasies; (2) removing masks of hypocrisy in order to be your authentic self; (3) thinking conceptually (that is, abstractly not just concretely as in childhood) about intellectual concerns; (4) preparing for self-sufficiency and independence once you are away from the support and guidance of parents; (5) handling differences with family members, teachers, dates, friends, and bosses on the job without blowing up; (6) internalizing your own, rather than imposed, beliefs, values, and standards of behavior; and (7) forming meaningful relationships with the opposite sex. Here, I am thinking of intimacy with another (more profound than the capacity to have sexual relations) without fear of loss of your unique self.

Part of your rebellion and your parents' response is positive. You push against those whom you love in order to test the boundaries, to determine at last who you are.

It's About Costly Mistakes. We smile when someone goofs, shrugs off embarrassment, and says, "You can't win 'em all!" And you can't. One can endure minor messes. For example, Steve, visiting with his date in a friend's house, slipped on the highly polished floor, scraped the floor with his shoe heel, and fell into an expensive piece of furniture. No bones were broken. Damages to the house were minor. The worst hurt was Steve's pride.

The bigger the blunder the harder feelings and reactions are to handle. A sixteen-year-old boy who has just completed driver's education naturally wants to drive the family car on dates. If he runs a stop sign and gets smashed by a stunned adult, he's had it. Or if he careens into a child on a bicycle and the youngster is hurt seriously, it may affect the youth for life. His career as a driver is altered by experience.

It's one thing to wreck the family car on a date or shopping trip. But it's quite another to take (steal) an automobile from a parking lot and go for a fast spin with a friend. A damaged fender can be repaired, but anyone who breaks the law is asking for trouble.

Some blunders appear stupid. The fourteen-year-old boy who stowed away in the wheel cradle of a jet airliner was trying to escape a bad home situation. He attempted to cross the ocean without paying passage and obtaining a passport. Instead, he fell two hundred feet to his death when the wheel bays opened. You sense that some deeds are heroic; others tragic; some are absurd.

"I wish that I had read that book on birth control (Alan F. Guttmacher, M.D., *The Complete Book of Birth Control)* six months ago," said a beautiful, pregnant seventeen-year-old girl. She was a most unhappy person, and I was trying to help her make the most of a bitter experience. "I didn't know a thing about contraceptive products, and Al (her boyfriend) didn't use anything." Deeply depressed, she looked out the window toward the river, as though it beckoned her, and said: "Sometimes I wish I were dead!"

That young lady is happily married today. Her child was adopted by a wonderful couple. Yet emotional scars that she and her family will never outgrow remain.

We injure other persons or damage private or public property at our own risk and peril. Smoking a cigarette or drinking beer is not the same thing as setting fire to one's high school. Arsonists are treated differently by society than smokers. Laws include rebellious students.

It's About Forgiveness. Like hypocrisy, unforgiveness is a terrible load to bear. The ordeal of being young would become unbearable without forgiveness and fresh starts. If we had to pay for every error in ruinous guilt feelings, pounds of flesh, and fears of future punishment, life wouldn't be worth it.

Really, we know that life cannot be reversed nor stopped, except by death. You can never recapture childhood's innocence. Yet life need not be destroyed by one sorry episode.

A father once said: "I only hope that when John and Bill (his small sons) are grown they will say, 'Dad did his best,' and forgive my failures. Parents aren't perfect. But my errors will be mistakes of the head, not of the heart."

Holding grudges can be expensive. It can divide families, even destroy personality. We need help to get back on the track and start moving. Sometimes, such care is the listening ear of a friend who can help sort out our crazy ideas from the healthy ones. Be willing to test out your ideas and feelings with someone you trust. Members of a family under stress can grow through sharing with a trained professional person who can help them find a wise course to follow. And God understands. It's not that he has to draw you a detailed picture of what he wants for your life. It's just that he knows your name and the shape of your struggle. That God cares helps a lot.

Stranded in the present? Making the most of today? Right! Even when you try your best—on an exam, a date, a job, in a game—you may not excel. The experience might be a flop. That's when you will want to stay in bed, pull up the covers, and have a big sleep. We learn, fortunately, even when losing. A manufacturer said engineers tried over a hundred thousand designs before perfecting a tiny flashcube. You have a legitimate complaint if parents preach instant perfection for ten minutes after you've goofed.

You need to see things in a bigger perspective to understand what you're up against. Are you old enough to run your own life, to get out of the family nest? Let's see.

3
Breaking Out of the Shell

You who can scarcely tolerate the old will find, as we have done, when you have come half circle, it becomes your portion to endure the young.

(Antonina Canzoneri, *Letter Home*, Broadman Press, 1959)

Sixteen-year-old Dana's relationship to her mother and father, grandmother, and world around her reflects the complicated perspective of her age. Here, we recreate the setting of a TV movie: "The Survival of Dana."[5]

Dana was the leading character in a story of post-divorce adolescents and antisocial behavior of some Southern California youth. Born in Fargo, North Dakota, Dana was pushed out of her family nest prematurely. It is tough finding one's way through the complex maze of growing up with parental understanding and support, let alone going through the grief of family disorganization. When her parents decided to divorce, Dana left her North Dakota home to live with a grandmother in Southern California.

Nicknamed Fargo, because of her origin, Dana (or Fargo) found her way into a mixed group of teenagers. She experienced them as rebellious toward authorities in school, home, and community. Interestingly, as an outsider, she felt the most acceptance from a band of upper middle-class kids who recruited her as an attractive addition to their unique clique. She and the owner/driver of a van became sweethearts. He was from a single-parent family and had a physically handicapped older brother, a war veteran. Two misfits—young, unhappy, unwanted, rootless, unemployed—were particularly vulnerable to each other's needs. They both needed parent substitutes but did not have them. With parental failure as a major common bond, they sought acceptance in a gang. Many young people like Dana are anxious, alienated, disappointed in themselves or their parents, and desperately hungry and groping for love, approval, and guidance.

Some youth break out of the shell with ease and grace. They are secure, feel loved, and seek to be launched with full family blessing and support. For others it is harder.

Dana and her friends provide a clue to what some American teenagers do after dark. They played high risk games with auto theft, vandalism, and plunder of people and property. Such youth are easy marks for cult leaders, paranoid gang members, and criminal characters who provide their followers alternative goals and rewards in the form of group acceptance. In the end, Dana's boyfriend, an essentially good guy, was gunned down by an enemy gang member. The "Christ figure" was killed and his best buddy ended up in a psychiatric ward. Dana regained her senses and came to honest terms with her grandmother, but the wounds of experience still lingered.

Revolt and Conformity

Teenage revolt and conformity are inherent in the process of becoming a person. To feel that no one wants you, no one cares about you, no one understands you—this is the worst kind of suffering. Unless someone recognizes you, respects your nonconformity, and permits you to do your thing, you feel alone. In fact, it can be so maddening that you feel like running away or committing suicide.

Is there any guidance for a teenager paralyzed by a helpless feeling of not mattering, of not really being, with other persons? What is involved in getting out of one's protective family nest and trying one's wings in free flight?

Experience has shown that this is what it's like for most young people. Freedom doesn't come all at once. Rather, one earns adulthood in several stages of development. Compare your experience with this process view of human growth.

Each child born into a family experiences three developmental phases in relation to parents. *In childhood* boys and girls depend upon others to make a place in the family circle for them and to provide for all their needs. Without a place and provisions secured, life is problematic. If one cannot belong to his or her own people, where does he or she fit into life? With too much conflict or control, however, one is not free to grow.

During early adolescence there is reshuffling among brothers and sisters in order to find a relatively secure position within the family. We should feel "at home" with our relatives, else we are "dis-eased." "I have spent some sad years with a feeling that I was not in my right place at the right time," said one person. Some teenagers leave home prematurely, because of hunger for a conflict-free environment. Others are victimized by closed family systems, physical abuse, and broken homes.

The *middle* and *late adolescent* is concerned primarily with breaking out of the protective shell provided by his parents. Tangible concerns for boys include: a driver's license, a car, a healthy body, girls, and education for a career. Late teenage girls think especially about: fashion, college, a career, and/or marriage.

Psychologically, you should progress through three stages: (1) *dependence* upon powerful providers; (2) gaining *independence* from family attachments and controls; (3) moving from alienation to *interdependence* with parents and adults. Your parents teach you to walk, then to walk away from them as you mature. In time, given good mental health, you are able to go home again—this time, a man or woman not a child. Meanwhile, how do you make peace with your parents?

Making Peace with Your Parents

Have you ever felt the ambivalence that one boy expressed? "What gives parents and teachers the idea that pressuring a young person will help him 'find himself'? They push off many unnecessary responsibilities on us. We need more time just to get to know ourselves." When the time comes to start "cutting the apron strings" nothing that parents do or say seems right in teenagers' eyes. The opposite may also be true.

Parents can be overbearing, even rejecting. Being kicked out if you don't get out is interpreted as family rejection. Communication (or the lack of it) becomes a problem. Sometimes parents just aren't there when you need them. As Jim said: "I can't talk to my parents. They are out of it and don't know what I feel. Neither of them is very religious. Did you have Christian parents? You were lucky. I cannot talk with them. I wish I could."

How can you work things out at home if you and your parents vibrate on different wavelengths?

One, admit your ambivalence. You have some capabilities and some limitations. You don't have to be free overnight, but you're in the process of gaining freedom from family controls. You still need love, money, approval, understanding, some guidance, and encouragement from significant others.

Two, watch how you rebel. It is possible to exalt your own ego to such a degree that you lose touch with people that matter, like parents. This was Paul's problem. He got into a fight at home and hit his mother. Later, reflecting upon the experience with a friend, Paul admitted his anger and alienation.

PAUL: The worst is yet to come, Bob. I hit mother tonight.

BOB: Paul! . . . Why? What happened?

PAUL: I just hit her, and I'm not sorry!

BOB: Back up. What happened?

PAUL: It started this morning. She started nagging me before I got up. She came storming into my room and told me to get up. I told her that my semester exams were over and that I didn't have to go to work until noon. But she made me get up anyway. (*Pause.*) As soon as I got home tonight, she jumped on my back again—just nagging. Finally something snapped and I jumped up from the supper table and just hit her—on the shoulder.

BOB: What did your dad do?

PAUL: He did not do anything at all! (*Pause.*) Well, he told me to calm down. I started to hit him, too.

BOB: What did your mother do?

PAUL: Nothing! She was too surprised.

BOB: Had you ever attacked your mother before?

PAUL: I've never hit her before, but I've hit my dad lots of times.

BOB: What would he do when you hit him?

PAUL: He would hit me back.

BOB: When did all this lick-swapping begin?

PAUL (*reflectively*): When I was thirteen and Todd was fifteen, Dad got a traveling job. He was gone a lot—sometimes two weeks at a time. We decided that we would start making our own decisions; so we did.

BOB: This is when the trouble started?

PAUL: I guess so. Mother didn't always agree with our decisions, and Dad certainly didn't agree with all of them. We were too big to whip, so he would just hit us. After awhile we started hitting him back.

BOB: What a surprise! An outsider would think you had a perfect home situation.

Anger can destroy a family or it can become a way to show concern. Because parents and teenagers experience a lot of tension, we will discuss anger later in some detail. Paul's experience warns us about verbal attacks, insults, and explosions. We need to express deep feelings effectively.

Three, learn to cope with overcoercion. According to psychiatrist Hugh Missildine, author of *Your Inner Child of the Past,* overcoercion is the most common parental attitude in our culture. When you were small, for example, you likely received a lot of bossing from grown-ups. Mother's carping still echoes in your ears: "If you'd get up ten minutes earlier you'd be on time for breakfast! Did you make your bed? It's late. Hurry! Your breakfast is getting cold. Don't forget to brush your teeth. You're going to be late for school!" Does that sound familiar?

You may still carry a chip on your shoulder from your "drill sergeant" father's commands: "Stand up straight. I don't want to have to call you again. Get off that phone! Will you shut up and get to bed!"

Adults try to prove that they are good parents by constantly directing and redirecting their childrens' activities. Some mothers and fathers expect their sons and daughters to make better grades, achieve more honors, and contribute more in life than they ever did. Meanwhile, children resist coercive directions by stalling, procrastinating, daydreaming, even avoiding contact with the "drill sergeant." What can you do?

Try to see your parents' orders (suggestions, ideas) as a form of anxiety about you and their own adequacy. They don't intend to paralyze you with a daily barrage of duties. Parents need to learn how to free you for self-starts, inner directions, and accomplishments. Deciding what you really want to do and abandoning their lists of "shoulds" and "have tos" will lower your resistance and increase your self-confidence.

True, you may stir parental disapproval when you defy their directions. But you can assert your individuality (ideas, tastes, styles) without losing both parents. Excessive adult pressures are relieved as your strength and self-esteem grow. Meanwhile, we all recognize that some gaps are real.

Some Gaps Are Real!

Adults are tempted to oversimplify your struggle. "Aren't kids basically the same as we were when we came along?" a father reasoned in a parent group discussion. The answer is: "No, because today's world is not the 1940s world."

The Generation Gap. Youth struggles for autonomy and independence. Clay wants a set of keys to his own car someday. Millie values style and wants freedom to wear clothes like other girls, to enjoy the "in" look. Money is the key to an adolescent's life-style. The capital of youth is *cash,* of young adulthood is *time,* and of mature adulthood is *energy.* Thus the generations' values differ.

Money liberates teenagers who control upwards of $30 billion worth of family purchasing in addition to their own spending money. Response to questions on how teenagers feel when shopping reveals that spending is an expression of independence. Youth buys not so much material things—cosmetics, records, cars, soft drinks, TV sets, clothes, cameras—but adulthood.

You are a member of a self-contained youth society. You establish your own values, lingo, styles, and skills. You enjoy liberties and luxuries that adults find hard to understand. You *are* breaking out of the shell!

The Education Gap. Everybody's heard of the new math, new biology, new English, and new physics, but not everyone understands that an educational revolution is going on.

Today's television child, says Marshall McLuhan, author of *Understanding Media,* stays tuned to up-to-the-minute adult news—inflation, politics, sex, taxes, crime, energy shortages, as well as to old adult movies. He learns fast from instant, *soundaroundus* communication.

Education was once restricted to mother's lap, father's knee, Sunday School lessons from the Scriptures, and uncomplicated primers. Learning, long associated with the glum, now is fun, action-packed, colorful, involved, and universal. The family circle has widened. Character no longer is shaped by two earnest, fumbling parents. Now all the world's a stage. Gaps of intelligence, information, and values are growing. Machines tell men what to believe, think, and do!

The Communication Gap. An insightful high school newspaper editor once commented on the need for parents and teenagers to get through to each other. He wrote:

"Today especially kids need to feel free to talk with some mature person whom they can trust. Normally you would think that this should be the parent, but it seldom is.

"Kids talk about their likes, dislikes, problems, wrong-doings, plans, desires, and loves among themselves. The reason being that they feel their parents won't understand. For the most part they are right."

He pointed out, I think correctly, that those persons with the greatest problems come from broken homes, homes where the father or mother is consistently absent from the family circle, and from homes where parents are so strict (conservative) that the child has never really had an opportunity to be himself or herself.

What do you think of this criterion of an effective home, worded as a double question? "Do the members of your family like to go home? Having been there for a while, do they like to get out?"

The person who asked that continued: "The 'good' family is seen as one which, through its capacity for sympathetic understanding and support, for warmth and closeness, pleasantry and fun, resolves frustrations, releases tensions, and sends its members—junior and senior—back to the bigger world again" This, of course, is the ideal.

The word "home" produces unique responses—from contempt to grateful praise—in family members. One girl recalled that her mother took her to every funeral in their small town, then expected her to look at each corpse after the service. She hated that experience; each occasion provoked resentment. It took years, plus psychotherapy, before she accepted her mother. Do you know anyone with a holdover hang-up like that?

"Home is the place where, when you have to go," wrote Robert Frost, "they have to take you in." You are fortunate if home is the place where you are loved, accepted, and understood.

4
On Becoming a Person

For every youth and maiden who is not strictly secluded or very stupid, adolescence is a period of distressful perplexity, of hidden hypothesis, misunderstood hints, checked urgency, and wild stampedes of the imagination. (H. G. Wells, *Joan and Peter*)

Entering life—making sense out of it and doing something with it—requires much more of us than exiting from it. Growing human personality is like constructing a great building. It takes much longer to acquire property, finance the deal, design and construct a building than to destroy one. We hear occasionally of some grand old structure in an American city that has been razed so that a new one can be erected. Such was the case with a seven story, eighty-six-year-old building, covering a square block of valuable downtown property, which was reduced to a pile of rubble in seconds. The victim of 500 pounds of well-placed dynamite, the building crumbled under its own weight when the explosives were detonated.

For a little child to make his or her way into the world, form a healthy personality, survive adolescence, and enter adulthood requires love, skill, patience, tenacity, and desire. One of life's most fulfilling moments occurs when a couple's first child is born. Yet, each step on the child's way to maturity offers grounds for frustration and fulfillment, for himself and his family. It is to the risks, relationships, and responsibilities of becoming one's own man or woman that our attention now turns.

Before you leave on a journey, it makes sense to consult a road map to discover different routes to your destination. If life were no more complicated than a jet flight to London, a computer could do your thinking for you. During childhood you are forced to follow directions established by your parents. They keep the map and read the road signs for their children. But youth on the spot need a road map, too.

Take Matthew's experience. "Somehow I seem depressed. I don't know what I'm doing. You are always happy; you don't worry. I never see you depressed. I'm not like all these happy people around here. I can't keep up with them. What can I do? What is the cause of it?" Some young people are forced to overcome major handicaps. Their psychological or physical suffering makes them feel different from other teenagers.

Some young people agonize without a guide. This book attempts to provide a kind of road map of the territory today's teenagers travel. A road map is not a route. Each individual must chart his own particular course. But a map does suggest different routes one may travel to reach his objective. Thus, I cannot say in simple, self-help fashion: "This is your ticket. Follow these steps and you'll run into no difficulties." That would be dishonest. You must be free to fail or succeed.

For people who are not ashamed of having brains, here are some basic concepts to assist in charting life's travels. I shall address you as God's person. If, perchance, you are not a professing Christian, here's hoping that you will think seriously about a life of faith and forgiveness. Feel free to discuss these ideas and how you feel about them with someone you trust. Now, what is becoming a person all about?

How It All Began

There are various views about how our universe and life in it began. Many scientists advocate naturalistic theories about the cosmos—how planets appeared in space, life began, and so on. Life for them was not created by God. Rather, it emerged through millions of years of evolution, mutations of species, and survival of nature's sturdiest creatures. A physiologist, commenting on experiments with laboratory animals and human subjects, disavowed man's uniqueness thus: "Tissue is tissue." For him, and many others, there is nothing special about human personality. The Bible teaches that man is much more than a stimulus-response machine or mix of molecules.

The Gift of Freedom. Genesis' early chapters report God's creating the heavens and earth, skies and seas, plants, animals, birds, and fish. When God created man in his own image, he became the steward or caretaker of all that God had made. It helps to view this creative process as a whole when we read: "God created man in His own image, in the image of God He created him; male and female He created them" (Gen. 1:27, NASB).[6]

God's *image* implies his own uniqueness—capacity to be, create, care for, and relate to his creation. Man's relationship to God's image is his ability to think, feel, relate, choose, and respond to God and other persons. He made us persons, not puppets, free to choose and responsible for our choices. Self-determination, rather than external compulsion, guides man in response to God's intention for him.

The Step from Innocence. Adam and Eve, God's first persons, were free to choose good or evil, to obey or disobey his explicit commands. Their life together was set in an idyllic place called the garden of Eden. While their setting was one of natural simplicity, their choices were real. They were both free to act and responsible for their behavior. When they disobeyed the Creator's instructions, by eating forbidden fruit and trying to take God's place, they lost the life they prized and were expelled from Eden. While the first persons on earth did not create evil, they had a capacity to choose either good or evil, to obey or sin (Gen. 2:16-17).

How did their disobedience occur? Did God make the first persons to sin? Does he blame us for what Adam and Eve did in the garden of Eden? The Bible pictures Satan as a tempting creature who raised doubt in Eve's mind about God's instructions. "You will be like God," he promised, creating a desire in her mind for the forbidden fruit. The couple's mutual disobedience followed with ruinous consequences—loss of their special relationship with God. This step from innocence caused both God and man to suffer. Man suffered alienation from his Creator. God suffered sacrificially by offering man forgiveness and redemption.

In Adam's fall, all creation was tarnished by sin and disposed to disobey God. This radical twist in human nature is what theologians mean by the term "original sin." The Bible notes that "everyone has sinned and is far away from God's saving presence" (Rom. 3:23, TEV).[7] By this statement the apostle Paul does not imply that we are guilty of Adam's sin, but rather of our own disobedience. Life after Adam's sin fell under the sway of sin and death. But thanks to God's love, he did not leave mankind without hope.

The Power of Forgiveness. God's relationship to you and me is remarkable. He made persons in his own image and gave them dominion over his creation. He trusted man's capacity to choose good, not evil, yet knew the risk of freedom. When Adam and Eve sinned, God searched for them and asked: "Where are you?" He still accepted them. Genesis 3:15 promised mankind a new beginning, with fresh power over Satan. Thereafter, the Old Testament tells of God's fashioning a nation, Israel, from whom his Messiah (Savior) would come.

We call the New Testament "good news" because it tells of God's great love for man. He made a way to forgive all sinful persons who trust him. John 3:16 tells us how this happens: "For God loved the world so much that he gave his only Son, so that everyone who believes in him may not die but have eternal life" (TEV). Human reason cannot explain God's provision for restoring fellowship. We can only accept his gift of forgiveness by faith. The apostle Paul affirmed, "By the free gift of God's grace are all put right with him through Christ Jesus, who sets them free" (Rom. 3:24, TEV).

This, according to God's Word, is how it all began. Such a record helps us to face reality and keep our priorities straight.

God is Creator; we are his creatures. He gives us just one time around in life, to make or break it. That's why it's so important to discover roots of personal identity.

Roots of Personal Identity

A college coed once said to a friend, "My parents gave me everything. But they forgot one important thing. They didn't tell me who I am." You may not be college age, but if you feel that you must find out who you are then you are more human than otherwise.

When a teenager asks, "Who am I?" he or she is confronted with depressing complexity—the desire to know, deny, and escape oneself. The girl above was becoming more aware of her identity. Life has a way of forcing each individual to integrate many emotions, impulses, memories, capacities, motives, and desires into one whole personality.

The psychoanalyst Sigmund Freud once said: "To be completely honest with oneself is the very best effort a human being can make." It is this effort at self-honesty which we now address. Take a case in point. Two sisters, sharing the same room, only two years apart in age may react in opposite ways to the identical set of circumstances. An argument, for instance, may drive one girl to tears, while her sister immediately pursues romantic interests by telephone. Why? We react to stressful situations almost automatically in a manner learned in an earlier stage of development.

You gain identity through a life-long process. Observations of primitive and civilized persons disclose something which safeguards the continuity of an individual's development. Psychologists call this "something" human identity—the dynamic synthesis, at any age, of one's unique self-perceptions. Identity is one's inner sense of sameness and continuity, through time, reinforced by significant persons, memorable events, key experiences, and social contexts.

Identity develops in chronological, definable stages. Erik H.

Erikson has advanced a concept of eight growth tasks that must be performed from infancy to late maturity. Each task becomes a growth crisis until it is successfully completed. Adolescence, for example, provokes the crisis of "identity formation versus identity confusion."[8] Here is where the struggle to become a person intensifies. A two-year-old's time is taken with learning how to walk, play, and put away toys. Whereas, teenagers are mastering harder tasks: sexual drives, school assignments, skin blemishes, part-time work schedules, dating, and so on. You are considered mature or immature according to your actions in each growth stage.

Becoming a healthy human being takes time. The decision to adopt a certain life-style—tough, intellectual, surfer, feminist, homosexual, straight—is seldom made all at once. You look for a hero or minihero to copy from competing models. You become, unconsciously, a composite of elements seen in others. Meanwhile, it's normal to have ups and downs. Perhaps you'd like all ups and no downs—an impossibility. We do reach plateaus of learning and satisfaction, however, and draw strength from placid days for stressful situations ahead.

Discover what fears you have about knowing yourself. You may have a friend who protects himself (from himself and others) by keeping his nose in a book, by working constantly, by sleeping, joking, or horsing around and never being serious. "In general this kind of fear is defensive," explains psychologist Abraham Maslow, "in the sense that it is a protection of our self-esteem, of our love and respect for ourselves."[9] Conversely, someone with low self-esteem, burdensome guilt feelings, or silly fears hides his true thoughts. Hypocrisy with yourself and those around you is a heavy burden to carry.

Talking with someone who matters helps to clarify ourselves. True, as one person said, "it is not easy to bleed in the presence of another person." If, however, that listener is skilled or wise or loving, he can help. He, like a good physician, would certainly do nothing to harm you.

"Sam is a good sounding board for me," admitted Cliff. "He's more conservative than I am but he lets me try out my wild notions on him without rejecting me." This sounding-board type person may be a parent who understands, a trusted teacher who cares, or a date who admires you. In the event of acute anxiety or depression you should see a competent counselor.

Our society has varied means—like extended college, technical schools, military service, even emotional illness—of granting delays to individuals who need more time before accepting adult commitments. Erikson calls such a strategic delay a "psychosocial moratorium," based upon his own experience as an art student in Europe and upon observing youths who postponed adulthood. Marriage may appear to be a way out of an unhappy home situation but may actually become a cop-out. With almost half of all marriages ending in divorce, the risk of repeating one's parents' marital mistakes is great. Many youth marriages are known to have resulted from illegitimate pregnancy. Such couples are on shaky ground from the start.

"I'm so mixed up, I don't know what I'm saying. Do you understand what I'm trying to say?" confessed a seventeen-year-old campus beauty. She may feel numbed by disappointments at home and frightened by pressures to perform now. Here's the rub. There are so many worries over premarital sex, grades, jobs, alcohol, drugs, and myriads of other problems that students aren't sure of anything anymore.

You know there is no such thing as "instant maturity," but, at least, you'd like a taste of significance.

A Taste of Significance

You have a way of becoming what you cherish devotedly and search for desperately. Right now, you may know more about what you dislike and don't want than something you do desire.

Two seventeen-year-old guys were talking about a fellow student's death following a motorcycle-car collision.

TED: Hollie, did you see that two-inch report in the back section of the paper about Tom's death? (Their buddy, Tom, ran into an automobile that pulled out from an intersection.) All they talked about were the funeral arrangements and his survivors! Nothing about Tom.

HOLLIE: Yeah, I may never be listed in *Outstanding Young Men of America* but I'd hate to get wiped out in an auto accident.

Both boys secretly longed for a taste of significance. The fleeting thought of dying in a motorcycle accident sobered them.

Your life-style today is shaped by the legacy of yesterday, plus the promise of tomorrow. You are what you have chosen from childhood and shall choose daily in the future. There is a poignant scene in the musical *Flower Drum Song* in which the aging Chinese father, Wang Chi Yang, tells his son: "Almost all of what you are up to now has come from me." Wang Ta, his late adolescent son, was eager to live his own life. In the process of achieving independence, however, sparks flew between Ta and his father.

If it is any consolation to you, struggles have always occurred between the generations. Parents and teenagers both grow in the process of maturing. Give your parents credit where it is due. You are more like them than you realize.

To repeat, you have a way of becoming what you cherish devotedly and search for desperately. What are the basic steps you will take to feel significant as a person?

Accept Your Physical Body. Next to your name, your body is your most prized possession. It clarifies your maleness or femaleness. Your body is a clue to how you feel about yourself—shame or pride. As your body grows and changes, you look for signs that the ugly duckling is turning into a swan.

With proper diet, exercise, and health care your acne will disappear, teeth may be straightened, and body will gain new, strong, and graceful proportions.

Your body and feelings about yourself are going to do a lot of changing in the years ahead. You'll have a lot of questions about what's going on: aspects of sexuality, health, nutrition, and effects of smoking, drugs, and liquor. You will find helpful answers in *The Teenage Body Book,* written by Dr. Charles Wibbelsman, a physician, and Kathy McCoy.[10] Or, you may prefer talking with your family physician yourself.

Accept Your Sexuality. Teenagers are tall and short, fat and thin, black, brown, and white, but, first and foremost—you are a male or female! Puberty, with its glandular rhythms, provokes profound physical transformations in young persons. Your attention and energies are absorbed with your "beautiful body," as one boy put it.

Guys experience rapid alterations in physique, which lead to comparisons with friends—height, body hair, feats of strength. Perspiration and acne concern both sexes. Overshadowing a girl's rounding hips and breasts is the onset of menstruation. A term used by some women for thier menses, "the curse," tends to convey, despite humor, the notion that menstruation symbolizes the female's burden and inferior status. Such is not the case. With proper preparation, a girl will feel proud (not ashamed) of her coming womanhood.

More or less accurate sex information becomes common knowledge at an early age—earlier than some adults imagine. Many parents are unwilling or unable to talk about sex with their growing, curious children. Some schools now instruct students in the meaning of sexual development. Books like *A Doctor Discusses What Teenagers Want to Know*[11] will answer many of your questions. Because so many unmarried teens are sexually active today, what you don't know *can* hurt you.

Form New Friendships. Youth are busy discovering their distinctive roles in United States culture, mid unisex pressures.

One disturbed, incredibly lonely boy asked, "What am I doing here, walking on this planet?" Many problems, noted researcher Merton P. Strommen, make some youth feel like psychological orphans.[12] They are propelled into loneliness over personal faults, lack of self-confidence, low self-esteem, poor classroom performance, concern over family pressures, shaky ties with the opposite sex, and anxiety about their God-relationship. What better reasons are needed for working on self-esteem and a warm interchange about mutual concerns with other people?

The burden of loneliness can become too great for some young people to bear. A girl on the way to womanhood needs befriending by competent parents and caring peers. A son needs the security of a true father's love as he achieves independence and his separate identity. Youth need special friends to help them negotiate life's tricky passages into adulthood. "Nonkindred family" persons in church fellowships can provide vital support groups, emotional strength, and guidance for growth. In *Take Care,*[13] I called this valuable help "the ministry of friendship."

Cut Some Ties with Parents. We have talked earlier about your changing relationship with your parents. You can be certain that they are experiencing "growing pains," too, as you struggle to mature. Your drive for independence and search for identity is made more difficult if your parents have only incompletely solved these problems themselves. Remember, they have parents, too. Your stormy periods may kick up old, unresolved issues in their personalities.

Search Out a Dependable Life-Style. Here, I am referring to the basic values, as well as external forms of behavior, that make you uniquely you. Life-style conscious individuals are searching constantly for models to follow. Once you have settled on the kind of person you wish to become—build a self-image you like—you fight to preserve it. Life-style's importance may be understood because it (1) commits us to a way of life; (2) communicates our identity to others; and (3) controls such choices as friends, work and play habits, religious preferences, and clothes and music tastes, as well as other decisions.

Exercise Your Options as a Teenager. You don't have full freedom yet, but you may have more privileges, opportunities, and possessions than some adults had at your age. You can prove your competence as a real person by helping with family chores, getting an education, and contributing to lives around you. A nonhostile way of gaining independence is working for pay. Another is by achieving athletic skill, mastering an enjoyable hobby, or learning to cook and sew.

Looking at the road map in summary, you cannot afford the luxury of waiting for tomorrow. A real person must live today. Using all available resources, identify your unique self, then opt for a taste of significance. With God's help, and that of Christian friends, you can make it.

5
Sex Is Here to Stay

Sex is who you are, not just what you do,

(C. W. Brister, 1979)

When we are young we expect sex to grow us up more than any other aspect of our lives. Our culture has made sex the be-all and end-all of existence. Boys grow up under the mystique of the hero man—lean, leathery, rugged, distant, and free. Girls grow up with a glamourous model image—passionate eyes, sensuous lips, clean hair, beautiful body, and proper clothes. Here you are, guys and girls trying to become persons in a society that hasn't decided for sure what it wants a man or woman to be.

Teenagers might paraphrase the ancient Greeks' view of the unknown god, "In sex we live and move and have our being." For the preteen and adolescent, sex is an anxious matter if not the only matter. Yet, in one's best moments, he or she knows that sex is not an end in itself. God's persons hold *agape* (giving) love, not sexual love, as the center of life.

No aspect of human experience consumes public affairs, the media and entertainment industries, personal and family relations, art and humor, and private emotions like sex. Sexuality is the small stage upon which life's most intense dramas are played. Yet, in many families, sex is the untalked about experience.

The Untalked About Experience

A metropolitan newspaper reported two stories involving human sex behavior the same weekend.[14] Physicians at

good" (Gen. 1:31). Contrary to what you may have been taught, sex is not bad unless it is perverted for evil purposes. God intended that sex be beautiful. Hence, personality is built or possibly destroyed through human relationships. Often, fantasies lead to perverted sexual practices.

Teenage Sex Fantasies

There is much misinformation going around about sex. A lot of teenagers say they can discuss almost anything except sex with their parents. There are still communications barriers about one's body, beliefs, and behavior to overcome.

Some young people refrain from asking their parents questions about sex for fear of making their parents think they are experimenting. An estimated four and a half million girls aged fifteen to nineteen are sexually active, along with their male partners. More than one million of these couples claim to use no contraceptives. Today's sexual freedom has left the burden of responsibility for contraception entirely upon women. Concern over health-related effects of the pill, plus sex education programs in schools, is beginning to reverse the trend.

Some parents possess less accurate sex information than their well-informed teenagers. Others are threatened by sex education courses in public schools. They think their kids are too young to understand it or, if they know the "facts of life," they'll do something wrong. Some parents falsely accuse their children by projecting flashbacks of their own guilt-laden past onto them. One mother, suspecting that her high school sophomore daughter was "giving in" to a boyfriend, dragged her down to the family physician. The doctor did a pelvic examination and reported : "Sue's not a virgin anymore, Mrs. Reid." Imagine Sue's relationship to her parents after that!

Because of concern with body image, peer pressure, high standards, violation of values, and self-esteem, sex is a stressful matter. Myths abound. Many girls fear that their breasts are too small, thighs too large, or face is ugly. Through menstruation they become sexual in an undeniable way. Still, many girls are confused about female anatomy and begin dating informed more by "old wives' tales" than accurate information. While boys's sexual equipment is obvious, the management of undeniable, dynamic sex drives and feelings remains a troublesome aspect of their lives. Driven underground by an adult conspiracy of silence and guilt over masturbation or overt sexual activity, youths lead double lives and suffer the burden of hypocrisy. Thus, we need to think about sex fantasies.

Omnipotence.—This is the magical notion that you have unlimited power, that all authority rests in your decisions, and that you are "free to live and free to die" with no thought of others. Such a person has intercourse with no idea of responsibility.

Indestructibility.—When a couple gives in and goes all the way, they think (again magically) that nothing can happen like pregnancy and veneral disease—that love will last forever. The story of a summer love affair between graduating high school seniors, called *Forever,* chronicles the fragility of boy-girl relationships. Cohabitation, rather than a go-ahead to sex without guilt, soon becomes a stroll down memory lane. Though they enjoy high risk sex games, unmarried players are never comfortable, at peace, about their illicit love. It's not like playing with dolls when one was three. Despite the "swept away" phenomenon, babies come from intercourse.

Peers know best.—Feeling that one's parents are too inhibited or poorly indoctrinated in their own generation's sex attitudes, most teenagers think that peers know best. One girl, aged ten, said of her closest friend—one year older than she: "I would have followed her through fire." As things transpired she did just that as they engaged in homosexual activities. Some gynecologists hold that a girl's peers are her best teachers in menstruation and management of sex behavior. Actually, one gets information from various sources: religious instruction and ideals, at school, from peers, reading, films, parents, and the tough business of growing up. Parents do basic and long-lasting sex education of their children, whether or not they do it well. Their model of respect, comradeship, attentiveness, fidelity, and mutual care rubs off for a lifetime.

Land of plenty.—A movie, *The Game,* portrays free love in a land of plenty. Peter is an adolescent and a virgin. At eighteen, virginity is often a demerit pointing against a guy with so many willing girls around. The game is to prove his manhood by becoming a player—getting a girl to give in. The male ego demands that he win the contest and dominate his sex partner. Nicky, his girl friend, let Peter "score" on a dare. Pressured by their peer group, Peter and Nicky found more than they bargained for. Free love is seldom free.

There are price tags of secrecy, over-possessiveness, dishonesty, shame, and fear. The suspicion, "Am I being used?" is always there.

"You don't know what it's like to be depressed, scared to death, and angry until you're in a home for unwed mothers," a nineteen-year-old confessed. Sex is everywhere in a land of plenty. Still, the stakes are high and risks are great.

Neutrality.—We have noted magical thinking among students whose distortions of reality can cause trouble. Distortions like: "I am god; nothing can happen to me!" And, "Everybody else does; why shouldn't we play, too?" The last fantasy I shall mention is the view of sex as a neutral, uninvolving experience.

"Sex is like brushing your teeth," argued one boy, "or eating food. One should do it as much as possible to avoid harmful side effects." (Do you suppose he meant something like cavities?) Such a person avoids commitment in sex acts and views the human body as a convenient piece of plumbing.

There's only one thing wrong with this fantasy. It isn't true! Intercourse takes on the quality of commitment, whether or not you intend it so. The eighteen-year-old girl who said, "I've used sex to hold people" is much nearer the truth. Modern females want a male who excites them, yet who cares. Wouldn't it make you feel cheated to lose out on love to someone who says, "Sex is like brushing your teeth?"

Sexual relationships, secure within marriage, are fulfilling and committing. A girl never forgets "my first love," with whom she had a serious relationship. On the other hand, without love, sex can be menacing, a potential destroyer, producing extreme anxiety and guilt feelings. One may conclude that we live in a complex time, where good and bad are mixed together. Traditional values still guide many American teenagers, though admittedly morals are changing.

Morals Are Changing

"There are still some morals around," suggested a sixteen-year-old girl, "but they are changing." Any period of rapid social change results in considerable confusion and distress on the part of people who are used to having rules set out for them. I have argued for sex within marriage, yet you are justified in reasoning, "With a forty to fifty percent divorce rate, how 'fulfilling and committing' is married love?" The divine ideal is still true, "What therefore God has joined together, let no man separate" (Matt. 19:6, NASB). Jesus Christ opposed an attitude of nonchalance and carelessness about the marriage bond. He challenged the easy divorce practices of the first century (Matt. 19:1-12) and advocated the permanence of marriage. While moral fads shift, basic Christian values remain.

I can't say how teenagers in general feel about premarital sexual relationships. But here is a classic insight into the subtle sexual psychology of one girl. *Playboy* morality to the contrary, Shirley reminds us that sex is a function of the whole person, not one part of the body alone.

After intimacies with Paul, who entered military service, Shirley said: "We were all right until we got close. I don't know . . . but something happened. After we did it three or four times, we started fussing. Since then, we haven't cared for each other. I don't even want to see Paul when he comes home on leave." She was frightened both by the possibility of pregnancy and of rejection. Shirley wondered: "Will the same thing happen with the next guy I date?"

Morals are changing, but the girl still gets stuck with the pregnancy as this letter to *Teen* magazine reveals.[16]

Jimmy and I couldn't wait so now we are married. Big deal!

Let me tell you what it is like to be married at 17. It is like living in this dump on the third floor up and your only window looks out on somebody else's third floor dump.

It is like coming home at night so tired you feel like you're dead from standing all day at your checker's job. But you don't dare sit down because you might never get up again and there are so many things to do like cooking and washing and dusting and ironing. So you go through the motions and you hate your job and you ask yourself, "Why don't I quit?" and you already know why. It's because there are grocery bills and drug bills and rent bills and doctor bills, and Jimmy's crummy little check from the lumberyard won't cover them, that's why!

Then you try to play with the baby until Jimmy comes home. Only sometimes you don't feel like playing with her. But even if you do, you get this awful feeling that you are only doing it because you feel guilty. She is so beautiful, and you know it isn't fair to her to be in that old lady's nursery all day long. Then you wash diapers and mix formula and you hate it, and you wonder how long it will be till she can tell how you feel, and wouldn't it be awful if she could tell already?

Then Jimmy doesn't come home, and you know it's because he is out with the boys doing the things he didn't get to do because you had to get married. So, finally you go to bed and cry yourself to sleep telling yourself "Why does he hate me so?" And you know it is because he feels trapped, and he doesn't love you anymore, like he said he would.

Then he comes home and he wakes you up, and he starts saying all the nice things he said before you got married. But you know it is only because he wants something, and yet you want to believe that maybe it is the old Jimmy again. So you give in, only when he gets what he wants, he turns away and you know he was only using you once more. So you try to sleep but you can't. This time, you cry silently because you don't want to admit that you care.

You lie there and think. You think about your parents and your brothers and the way they teased you. You think about your backyard and the swing and the tree house and all the things you had when you were little. You think about the good meals your mother cooked and how she tried to talk to you, but you were so sure she had forgotten what it was like to be in love.

Then you think about your girl friends and the fun they must be having at the prom. You think about the college you planned to go to, and you wonder who will get the scholarship they promised you. You wonder who you would have dated in college and who you might have married and what kind of a job would he have?

Suddenly you want to talk, so you reach over and touch Jimmy. But he is far away and he pushes you aside, so now you can cry yourself to sleep for real.

If you ever meet any girls like me who think they are just too smart to listen to anyone, I hope you'll tell them that this is what it is like to be married at 17!

Yes, there is a sex revolution underway in our world. Some things needed to change—like men owning women as their property, like the tribe of Africans who once crucified women for committing adultery, like forcing adolescent girls to submit to a crude form of clitorectomy in order to deaden sexual response, and like circumcising boys at puberty largely to discourage masturbation. Marriages arranged by ancestors needed to go. A double standard—separate sex codes for men and women—should disappear from the earth.

Old appeals are gone. Yet, enduring foundations to guide sexual decision-making and sustain family life are essential.

How Do You Decide?

While the Bible does not tell us all we *want* to know about sex, courtship, masturbation, incest, birth control, artificial insemination, sterilization, abortion, and perversions like homosexuality, it tells us all we *need* to know for responsible sexuality.

What does the Bible say about sex and marriage? It offers enduring principles, not specific rules, for decision making.

1. God has written maleness and femaleness into our natures. He called his creation "very good" (Gen. 1:31), and trained Adam and Eve for responsible freedom.

2. "To know" one's mate, in the biblical sense (Gen. 4:1), implies a deep, personal relationship—a life commitment. Sex is erotic, but also involving. Intercourse becomes a covenant of communication at life's deepest level.

3. Marriage, consummated by sexual union, needs to be entered freely—by personal selection of one's mate (Gen. 2:24). It is for the mature who are still growing.

4. Sexual love is holistic, not simple. This refers not only to your mate's complex mystery, but to the exclusiveness of marriage. God's intention is *one* man with *one* woman for life (Matt. 19:1-6).

5. The ultimate ground for sexual relations is fidelity. Once selected, one's life partner merits exclusive loyalty. Husbands and wives are dependent upon each others' faithfulness (Eph. 5:21-33).

There are plain prohibitions against sex outside of marriage, premarital and extramarital (Matt. 15:18-20; Acts 15:19-20; 1 Cor. 6:18-20; 1 Thess. 4:3), along with the commandment: "You shall not commit adultery" (Ex. 20:14, NASB).

A conversation with sixty-two unwed mothers, ranging in age from fourteen to thirty-one, reminded me that many persons have missed the ideal mark. Many sufferers are enmeshed in tragic perversions of true love. It is not preventive guidance but powerful forgiveness and a new chance at life which they need. The Bible helps persons whose values have been violated to find paths of forgiveness and usefulness again.

Perhaps no biblical character is presented more graphically and humanly than Israel's king, David, the son of Jesse (1 Sam. 16:11-13). He was called "a man after God's own heart," yet committed adultery with Bathsheba and had her husband, Uriah the Hittite, killed in battle (2 Sam. 11:3; 12:24). While David shamefully sinned with Bathsheba, he knew how to repent. He confessed, "I have sinned" (Ps. 51:4, NASB) and pled for pardon.

God does not take such pleas for acceptance lightly. "If we confess our sins to God, he will keep his promise and do what is right; he will forgive us our sins and purify us from all our wrongdoing" (1 John 1:9, TEV). The spirit of Christ is not to condemn but to save (John 3:17-21).

You are tempted to decide sticky issues by statistics, the fear of being disliked, and craving for popularity. Here are some helpful bases for decision-making.[17]

One basis for deciding about sex is possible outcome.—What happens as a result of sexual relations? Something good or something bad? Your decision should be based upon possible outcome in terms of your own values. Ask: Whom will I hurt? A little selfishness helps: Will it be myself?

Another basis for moral decision is that of universality.—Ask yourself what it would be like if everyone did just what he or she felt like. If every boy took any girl who was available, what assurance would they have of fidelity after marriage? Where are the limits in a "bed now, wed later" world?

A third basis for developing premarital sex standards is cultural.—Unrestricted sex could occur only in a society (1) providing sex education in contraception, (2) where there were no prohibitions, (3) no feelings of guilt and shame, (4) if privacy were readily available, (5) if venereal disease were rare or nonexistent, (6) where provisions were made for all illegitimate offspring, (7) where religious sanctions approved premarital sex, and (8) where free love promoted family life. Such a culture, in fact, is nonexistent.

"Why wait?" A fourth practical idea.—Who wants to be a loser at fifteen or seventeen, a time which is already shaky? Virginity, despite changing attitudes, makes a boy or girl more desirable. If you flunk on the second date, more than morality is at stake. You may lose your self-esteem, virginity, and opportunity (later) to marry someone you like. As a teenager said, "Sex can ruin a beautiful friendship."

To summarize, psychiatry and religion agree that men and women are made for each other. Happily, sex is here to stay. You hear a lot of fascinating, yet fictitious, stories of couples in and outside of marriage. I call them sexual fantasies.

True, people need people all the time, everywhere. Our society provides appropriate channels for sexual expression according to one's maturity and marital state. At seventeen, it's more fun to have a date than a mate. Be true to your standards. If you're one of the many millions of teenagers who don't—then stop apologizing! Sex is great. Is it great enough to save for your marriage?

6
Discovering Your Purpose

> We need a theme? then let that be our theme: that we, poor grovellers between faith and doubt, the sun and north star lost, and compass out, the heart's weak engine all but stopped, the time timeless in this chaos of our wills—that we must ask a theme, something to think, something to say, between dawn and dark, something to hold to, something to love.
>
> (Conrad Aiken, *Time in the Rock*)

Where are you headed in this hang-loose, gotta-have-a-gimmick world? Do only persons with good looks, real brains, and a lot of money make it? Getting your bearings—finding your place in adult society—may be described in one word: *tougher.*

As you explore the horizon of your brief span of history, you sense that the world is large enough to become lost in. "Never before," said a high school senior, "have we faced so many uncertainties. You can't count on anything staying the same." We are in the midst of a time described by Teilhard de Chardin as the "coming awakeness" of man. Futurist Edward B. Lindaman has pictured this period of history as an "uneasy adolescence," a time of confusing new feelings and fears. We must prepare faithfully for the future. "Our real education," says Lindaman, "is in the mystique of the hot knife of technology as it slices through flesh and blood, and the blunt hammering of personal and impersonal traumatic events on the fragile human spirit."[18]

You sense that unless a person possesses a clear grasp of reality, well-defined values, and priorities he or she faces big difficulties. The unprepared adolescent experiences growing confusion and uncertainty. As the pace of change quickens, a purpose becomes imperative.

Even small victories are welcomed. A bright young secretary in a large firm came home from work one evening and sighed, "I really accomplished something today."

"Got a big job out of the way?" responded her father.

"No," she replied. "I found out that all the auditors are married." At least she knew where not to look for a date.

Becoming an adult does not free you from decisions. It increases your responsibilities and makes you vulnerable to even more options. You cannot live forever between twelve and twenty. Little Orphan Annie stays small for forty years only in the comic strip. Sooner or later Winnie the Pooh and the Paddington Bear give way to deeper things—lessons from Shakespeare, lab practicums in organic chemistry, earning a living, auto accidents, production lines, sickness, and death. Whatever happened to the simple secure world of childhood?

As you search out life's options and opportunities, inevitably you will discover that everything isn't OK.

Everything Isn't OK

Adulthood has a way of foreclosing on adolescence. Friends pair off and marry. Loss of family ties leaves youth craving intimacy with someone who matters. Having a boyfriend, at seventeen, becomes desperately important for a girl. A guy can change courses or majors just so long. Eventually he must settle down and conquer a specific area of the vocational world. Can you say now, "I want to be a ____________"?

Ambivalence abounds. The end of adolescence is both exhilarating and depressing. According to one seventeen-year-old: "Everything isn't OK. We only stand on the edge looking over. We're ready to step into life, but not quite. It's awesome. It's pretty good. But it's terrifying! Why *do* we believe the things we were taught by our parents and the church? Is it enough just to be told what to believe?"

Teenagers seek an authority they can trust. One youth described gray areas of decision making thus: "Being a Christian is confusing. We face conflicting loyalties. For instance, all our lives our parents have taught us that personality is sacred. Abortionists come along advocating the taking of life as a safe, clean birth prevention procedure. We're taught to care for the earth, yet nuclear power plants pollute the environment. We need alternate energy sources. Who is right? Whom shall we obey?" There are conflicting loyalties.

Young people desire and deserve a chance to live. Yet when a youth unmasks, he admits to feeling lonely, out-of-it, driven either to succeed or be conquered by life. "I don't have any big problems," said a fifteen-year-old boy, "just a lot of little ones making life bad news." He elaborated on how it is to be young—without a job, car, money, girl, or family that understands. That's a white-Anglo-Saxon-Protestant view. What about the blacks?

Psychiatrists William Grier and Price Cobbs told in *Black Rage* what Negro youths face because of white America's assumption that black persons are unintelligent. Our culture has programed a black youth of above average intelligence to act clumsy, ignorant, and contemptible. This is white society's perception of its supremacy. It carries a high price tag of psychological and economic expense.

The black boy wonders: "Will I be smart, clean, clever, obedient, loved, successful, important, rich (and white), or will I be stupid, dirty, awkward, defiant, despised, and an unimportant, impoverished failure (who is black)?"[19] The premise of education must cope with the view projected onto blacks by whites and themselves. Changing humiliating prejudice is a fundamental social concern.

It's a pressure cooker world where one can make or break it pretty fast. Another way to spell it is *trouble.*

This brings the discussion around to you. Are you ready for life, but not quite? Where are you headed? Still looking for the road, or have you been fortunate enough to find it? The distance ahead looks like an immense journey, the traffic is heavy, your destination uncertain, and the time is late. Where are you headed, fast-driving friend? Do you have a purpose for life?

A Purpose for Life

When asked about his work opportunity at a government installation, a high school dropout replied: "I just fell into it. I've been doing the same thing for eleven months and am bored to death. My brother-in-law's gonna get me a job in the lumberyard where he works." Without a sense of direction one is a drifter, always dependent upon someone else to think and act for him. Is the main purpose of your life to (1) get more money, (2) get married, (3) stay in school as long as possible, (4) "work the minimum; get the maximum," (5) leave home, (6) survive, or what?

Psychologists generally agree that young people work best when they have a purpose, when they understand the reasons for their work. We are all headed somewhere, searching for a passport to life. Time pushes us along. Parents and teachers pull us aside, remind us to select some goals, and get our bearings. Affirmations come, like: "We believe in you" or "I know you'll amount to something someday."

More than a century ago Lewis Carroll pictured youth's need for purpose in *Alice's Adventures in Wonderland.* In one scene Alice speaks to the cat.

> "Would you tell me, please, which way I ought to go from here?"
> "That depends a good deal on where you want to get to," replied the Cat.
> "I don't much care where—so long as I get *somewhere,*" Alice added as an explanation.
> "Oh, you're sure to do that," said the Cat, "if you only walk long enough."

Alice might be the young woman who confessed, with hands over her face, "I'm so mixed up; I don't know what I'm doing." She might be experimenting with marijuana, with sex, with alcohol.

Alice, on the other hand, may be the idealist on your campus. She describes herself as "aware and concerned" about problems like energy, poverty, racial inequality, hypocrisy, ecology, and the urban crisis. You may think her "causes" are kind of sad. She hasn't learned that the human condition is not one of infallibility. She expects people to be perfect.

How can you find a purpose unless you know what it means? By *purpose* I imply a fundamental desire, direction of energies, and positive intention to make something of your life. A goal does not have to be stated in vocational terms, like: "I want to become a pilot" or "I plan a modeling career." Early vocational choices may border more on fantasy than reality. Your self-expectations, life-style, and idealized image of what you desire from life are wrapped in the purpose package.

Right now, your purpose may be stated negatively. There are some things—like contemporary values—you may wish to avoid.

Michael J. Sniffen, while a student at Princeton University, wrote: "A new breed of students has entered the nation's colleges. . . . They are not so much impressed with what their parents and their nation achieved as what remains for them and their nation to do."

New pathways lie ahead. Discovering your purpose is an unending process. It lasts through all the seasons of life. Amounting to something may force you to work against the odds.

Against the Odds

Take the experience of a young black girl, Wilma Rudolph, of Clarksville, Tennessee. Since her story of victory over poor health as a child was the subject of a movie, you may know of her fight against the odds. One of eight children in a poor, black, uneducated family, her achievements as an Olympic champion are even more remarkable.

Wilma ("Skeeter" as her family and friends knew her) was literally loved and challenged into a great purpose. Her parents did not spoil her but they recognized that she was special in several ways. Her mother inspired Wilma with discipline and determination. She wore a leg brace for years and could not play vigorous games with healthy children. Rather than taking the brace as a "cross" or penalty, one day Skeeter took it off and shot goals on the dirt basketball court at home. She learned to run, pivot, fake, and make accurate shots. A coach in high school recognized her potential. He recommended to her parents that she work with a Tennessee State University track coach the summer she was sixteen.

Overcoming great handicaps—physical, economic, psychic, and social—Wilma Rudolph was motivated to win sprint events in track meets. In 1956 she ran in the Olympic games in Melbourne, Australia; and, despite a serious moral failure (an out-of-wedlock child), won three gold medals in the 1960 Olympic games in Rome. I met and visited with this gallant young woman when she was about eighteen. Already a champion, it was evident that she had decided to make something of her life. Rather than bitterness toward God for her crippled beginning or hating the father of her child, Wilma was a winner.

One can always search for an excuse for failing in life—being crippled as a child, having an uneducated father or a dominant mother, or being one of eight poor children. We must watch such "outs" since most of us face crises along the way. Wilma Rudolph didn't have life handed to her on a silver platter. From a human point of view, her beginnings were bleak. Yet, her parents had great faith in God and a consuming care for all their children. Wilma's decision to make something of her life was actually a series of decisions. Unsatisfied with the traditional paths most of her peers took in Clarksville, Tennessee, she built an admirable life as a citizen of the world. Without glossing over her humanity and failures along the way, Wilma earned a nation's gratitude as its victorious representative in the Rome Olympics. She is still succeeding as a wife and mother.

Start Discovering Life Now

Wilma's experience may prompt you to discover life now, not "someday, when you're older." Some kids are geared to the present but not to planning. A girl attending a rock music festival said, "We're more oriented to the present. It's like do what you want to do now. . . . If you stay anywhere very long you get into a planning thing. So you just move on." Discovering your purpose is more than doing your own thing. You can escape reality just so long.

How can you tell the difference in a passing impression and the genuine leading of the Lord? We are invited to "wait upon the Lord" through prayer and find direction in his Word. We can associate with Christian friends, youths and adults, and talk with persons in whom we have confidence. Some doors open; others slam shut. God creates opportunities through what we call "providential circumstances" and guides us along.

Given this context, you will try to keep your purpose open, fluid, sensitive to the options ahead. Add to the *desire* to make something of your life the *faith* that you can shape your future. Can you state your search for a purpose in clear terms? If not:

Know that you are not alone. Others are in the same boat.

Open yourself to God and his will for your life.

Seek the best vocational guidance available in your school.

Find another person who needs you and be meaningful to him or her. Intimacy and identity run together in warm, human relationships. You can help each other to grow.

Discover the options open to you, as well as your basic gifts, talents, and capabilities. Life will make a place for you, but you must try to make a place for yourself.

Meanwhile, you might ask yourself:

1. Am I just holding my ground against my parents when differences arise, or am I progressing toward definite goals?

2. Do my parents treat me like a child because I act emotionally like a child? If I behave like a more mature person do they respect me more?

3. Do I exercise the right to make up my own mind on some questions without interference from anyone? Do these matters receive my best judgment or spur of the moment ideas?

4. Have I accomplished anything to be proud of this year? What recognition came when I chose responsibly?

5. Can I make up for my weaknesses by focusing on one major strength? You might pray: "Jesus, please help me put my efforts into something useful that will help me feel good about myself and close to you."

7
A Time to Decide

There is a tide in the affairs of men,
Which, taken at the flood, leads on to fortune;
Omitted, all the voyage of their life
Is bound in shallows and in miseries.

(Shakespeare, *Julius Caesar*, ACT IV, sc. 3)

Once on a trip out West our family visited scenic Oak Creek Canyon in Arizona. The highway descended dizzily as we negotiated hairpin curves and caught breathtaking views. We, who had been taller than the green aspens and firs, were soon surrounded by a forest of giant trees. Once on the canyon floor it was difficult to make sense of nature's wonderland. The arena was shadowed and vision shortened. It took ascending once again, pausing at a roadside park, and reflecting momentarily to enjoy where we had so recently traveled.

Students say that indecision is one of their top personal problems. Like the canyon floor darkened by the forest, life gets heavy without enough time, money, and decisiveness to go around. Drawing on many experiences, we now consider the challenge of decision making in several areas of life.

The Challenge of Decision

Part of growing up is choosing the right steps to take. The day comes when you walk away from your old oxfords in a new pair of heels, style your hair, get a job, or (perhaps secretly) smoke your first cigarette. Some decisions are easy; matters of conscience are harder. Deciding what to do with your life is quite complicated. It seems as big as an earthquake and almost as shattering if things don't work out.

"How can I choose my life work at seventeen?" asked Bill. "There are so many things to do and that need to be done."

Perhaps you know someone who decided early on to go to medical school, but he or she was never admitted. Now, they are making the most of life's "second best" in a career unrelated to medicine. Most persons, in fact, change jobs or careers several times before discovering what they really want to do.

The time of decision is upon you. The word *decide* comes from two Latin words which, taken together, mean "to cut off." To decide has a note of finality about it. It implies that one has determined and settled a matter. A conclusion has been reached. As a matter of fact, opening one door may lead to a hundred others not yet opened. You may feel like throwing up your hands in dismay over shaping your future. You feel powerless, living in a world of manipulators and impersonal forces, to control the kind of life you want. Strict control of your environment and circumstances (like neighbors' behavior, energy sources, violence, inflation, or war) is not possible. One decides with the light and resources available, then tries to make good on the choices reached.

There are many roads ahead, not all of an equal order: lifestyle, values, goals, friends, religious commitments, national issues, work, family, marriage, and the future. We want to consider some of them. Fortunately, God wants to help you face whatever life brings. Your family and friends, at their best, want you to make it, too.

Attitudes and Values

Basic to all other decisions in life are one's attitudes and values. One's attitudes relate closely to feelings and behavior. An *attitude* is a position taken or view assumed to suit a given purpose. Attitudes flow alongside needs and motives.

In checking attitudes, we might ask: Is one's position realistic or unrealistic, positive or negative, creative or destructive, esteem-building or guilt-inducing, peaceful or violent, supportive or demeaning, open or closed, accepting or prejudiced, joyous or angry, loving or insecure, principled or expedient, lawful or illegal? Or does one's view lie in a gray area, between the black/white alternatives pictured here? Attitudes eventually become life-giving forces or death impulses. They build or destroy.

Many attitudes, like one's motives, appear to lie out of reach of conscious control. We would like, at least occasionally, to blame someone else or circumstances for our attitudes and behavior. While you can hold no one (other than yourself) accountable for your feelings and attitudes, the people around you certainly influence your behavior.

In Wilma Rudolph's case, for example, she may have taken a grim, defeatist attitude toward life at an early age. She could have burned with rage, become a cynic, ended up chronically depressed as a psychiatric patient, or turned to drugs and violence. Being crippled, however, did not kill her spirit. Rather than turning against her seven sisters and brothers, they helped one another.

A *value* is an idea, ideal, person, or thing highly prized. The more one values something—a trip to Acapulco for instance—the harder one works to achieve it. Once a value is determined it serves as a point on a compass in guiding one's steps. One fights to protect values, like freedom in America, or to defend the rights of others. Values include intangibles, like respect for personality, faith in God, and telling the truth; as well as tangibles, like money, political office, or business success. Health is a primary value to most people.

If Wilma Rudolph had valued the best of everything, in material terms, for herself and her family, she would have capitalized upon her Olympic feats. Her behavior would have been different. She would have hired an agent, commercialized her name, endorsed products, made public appearances, and sought to marry into wealth or fame. Instead, she married her childhood sweetheart and settled quietly in a Tennessee city to rear her children out of the public eye.

Efforts at value clarification are underway in a number of schools,[20] but these educational and research projects usually make no attempt to teach basic Christian values. The church and home remain primary sources of attitude shaping and value formation in the United States. As we shall see in all other areas of decision making, the challenge of attitudes and values is crucial. One's basic positions influence goal-setting, life-style, choice of friends, religious beliefs, work, marriage, management of money, and the like. You are now and will become what you cherish devotedly and pursue avidly.

Life-style

You are already deciding the kind of life-style that you enjoy or imagine that you might enjoy—given the opportunity. A banker's son confessed, "I was reared with a silver spoon in my mouth and I enjoyed it." His family lived in a plush part of town, drove expensive automobiles, wore elegant clothing, enjoyed a luxuriously appointed house, traveled first class, stayed in the best suites at the best hotels, employed efficient maids and gardeners, and indulged in every conceivable luxury that money could buy. He grew up accustomed to the best of everything.

Were his parents exploiters of the poor, dishonest in business dealings, seeking to defraud the Internal Revenue Service of the United States with tax write-offs? Not really. Of course, his father knew how to handle the operations of a sizable bank, including visits by state and federal bank examiners, and the scrupulosity of auditors. He was careful with investments of zealous stockholders and kept an eye on corporate profits. The family employed able attorneys and lived within the limits (and full privileges) of the law. Upright church members and "first citizens" of their community, they enjoyed the advantages that wealth afforded.

On the other hand, I recall a beautiful girl who grew up among migrant workers. Her family lived in the back of a pickup truck, in barns, sheds, garages, cheap motels, or wherever they could find protection from the weather and privacy for meals and sleep. There was no guaranteed wage for her mother and father, who followed the potato harvest from the Southern states to Long Island, New York.

"I never knew where I'd be in school, " she related, "or if I would be in school. We moved seventeen times before I finished high school and followed the harvest in season."

Migrant families have no guarantees of good crops, medical care, top prices, new cars, education for children, and no promises of frills or luxuries. Virile young people burn out early—tired of being shoved, pushed, punched, and screamed at. They weep in the night for a better life. Such folk have no attorneys when confronted by the law, save a stranger from the Legal Aid Society or American Civil Liberties Union. Neglect dogs their tracks. They wait in line for government funded food coupons, for health care, for almost everything. Such is the plight of the poor.

That girl confessed, not to immorality, but to low self-esteem: "I feel like a pile of filthy rags thrown into some corner." Exhausted with running, a stranger to self-indulgence, she longed for a place to stop, people with whom she could relax, and a family to love her for her own sake.

Life-style is economic. It has to do with where one fits in American culture—with money, ego, and power—or poverty and powerlessness. It is also ethical. Life-style deals with how a person moves ahead in his or her surroundings and chosen field of endeavor. Some people choose to play life straight, conform to religious values, serve or assist other people, and work with great integrity. Others take shortcuts to success, flaunt morals, and follow the winds of expediency. These are the guys or gals in your school who cut into lines, push ahead impatiently, take advantage of other people's weaknesses, and operate on the edge of morality. They prize popularity and use people to their own advantage.

To be poor is not the moral equivalent of goodness. Many dismally poor persons are brutal, violent, thoughtless, and cruel. To be rich is not the moral equivalent of badness. Many wealthy individuals identify with society's underdogs, support helpful social causes, and are generous with their time and money. They are genuinely great, not evil, people. Often misunderstood, wealthy persons might be a community's loneliest residents.

Here is where the Bible helps us. It contrasts life-styles, not of the rich and poor, but of righteous and wicked individuals. The psalmist wrote:

> How blessed is the man who does not walk in the counsel of the wicked, nor stand in the path of sinners, Nor sit in the seat of scoffers! But his delight is in the law of the Lord, And in His law he mediates day and night. For the Lord knows the way of the righteous, But the way of the wicked will perish, (Ps. 1:1-2,6, NASB).

Following the writer's logic, a greedy wheeler-dealer, who appears to win (legally or not) in today's world, is an ultimate loser. He achieves success with dishonesty, views goodness with contempt, and confuses his desires with acceptable behavior.

You must decide how creative and productive or destructive and deceptive your life-style will be. Will you live a dog-eat-dog existence or care deeply about people? Do you want others to trust or distrust your leadership at school? Are you enthusiastic and confident or embarrassed and ashamed? Do you know or just pretend to know what you're doing? Do you feel good about yourself or all hollow inside? Must you live with a cheat or can you be real with people? A life-style choice is yours—given the measure of health and opportunity your situation provides.

In earlier chapters we have noted the urgency of teen decisions in areas like identity, family relations, sexuality, health care, and life goals. In chapters 8 and 9, the process of making three big decisions—career, college, and marriage—will be presented. It remains for us here to examine temptations that will come through the pressure to conform. "Everybody's doing it" is a standard human out (excuse) for often questionable behavior. Yet the urge to conform is real.

The Pressure to Conform

Conformity comes from two Latin words which, taken together, mean "to make or be like, to act in harmony or agreement." It refers to our quite normal desire to be like everyone else. "When in Rome, do as the Romans do" is the ancient permission given for conformity. Teenagers like what others their age like, fear what they fear, wear what they wear, say what they say, and think what they think. A conformist fears disapproval, thus feels a great need to be like everyone else.

A group places tremendous pressure on its members to belong, be like all other members, and accept their standards of belief and behavior. Decisions about agreement of disharmony with one's peers lie closely alongside one's life-style. If you know who you are, have a clear purpose in view, and are guided by strong biblical standards, handling peer pressure will come easier for you . Be warned, fitting in when "everybody's doing it" is easier than standing alone.

Advertisers understand the awesome power of suggestion. Liquid detergents are "in" and powdered soaps are "out," according to some public relations firms. We're told that the "dry look" is appealing; whereas, "the wet-head is dead" for men. Those who desire sex appeal, good looks, and approval avoid hair oil at all costs. Small cars are popular because of expensive and limited fuel. They are more economical to operate and maintain than big "gas guzzlers." Already *in* with many members of the young adult set, smaller vehicles will become a *must* for most Americans in the future.

No one wants to be disliked by his or her fellow students. Social rejection is crushing. You don't want to be teased, ridiculed, or laughed at. So you go along on clothing and hairstyles, places to eat, hit recording groups, brands of drugs and beauty aids, and likes and dislikes. You have friends who are highly suggestible, easily influenced by ideas, hints, and proposals from other persons. "I could never say no if Karen asked me to do something," confessed Carole. "It might hurt her feelings or she might think I don't like her anymore." In actuality, Carole plays it safe with Karen and others because of feelings of inferiority. She's afraid no won't stick and says yes, hating herself all the while.

One must feel good about himself to let his "Yes be yes and No be no," as Jesus Christ taught (Matt. 5:37). In fact, the entire Sermon on the Mount, in Matthew 5—7, is a call to authenticity. "You count and I count" is a thoroughly Christian affirmation. One who seeks to please God in all things does not "serve two masters." He does not try to please "God and mammon" (Matt. 6:24). When guided by great convictions like that, one can survive ridicule or fear of being disliked.

Courage to Say No. A boy told of leaving church with a group of guys after choir practice one mid-week evening. They were just driving around at night, looking for fun, when the driver pulled out a six-pack of beer and passed it around. Four of the five guys each took a can and popped the top. Mike, seated by the door, refused because he felt the alcoholic beverage would harm his body. His parents had recommended that he never take the first drink. So, without hesitation, he declined.

"Aw, come on, goody-goody," taunted Tommy from the back seat. "Whatsa matter? Is mama's boy scared? Are you afraid your daddy will find out?" Mike stood his ground, "I'd rather not."

"Who would have thought that Mikeie-Baby is a big chicken!" pressured Jim. "Come on, Mike. Try it, you'll like it!" Mike felt his face getting red. He was half-mad and embarrassed. The othe boys had begun to tease, too, so the pressure was enormous. His heart was pounding. The temptation to pop a top and give in was strong because, before that, he liked all the guys. He wondered whether or not they popped pills, too, and where else they "let the bars down."

Can you say no with the same courage Mike conveyed? He had decided long before the ride that night who he was and how far he would go in matters like sex, drugs, smoking, and alcohol. His health was a paramount value and he wanted to remain in control of his faculties. He knew that he did not want to get drunk on alcohol or high on drugs.

Winning Respect. Before the guys returned to the church parking lot that night, Frank admitted: "Mike, you've got guts. You're the only one of us who dared to be different."

Joe, the driver, joined in, "Yeah, we didn't want anyone to get hurt. We were just having a little fun. I must admit, at first I thought you were a stick-in-the-mud. Now, I admire your courage." Had Mike been a jellyfish and joined the beer drinkers on the joyride, he might have gained their approval but lost their respect.

How much better it is to show that you have confidence in yourself when the pressure is great. You can say, "You guys go right ahead, but beer's not for me. This whole thing is stupid!" The other fellows drank because they were afraid to be different. Mike proved that most teenagers respect a guy or girl who has the courage to say no. That individual knows who he is and knows what her limits are. Courage is the mark of true leadership. It wins friends among one's peers and appreciation from adults.

To repeat, the time of decision is upon you. Be patient with yourself as you learn to make decisions. You'll make mistakes; you'll win some victories. As a decisive young person, you'll help some friends to survive peer pressure, too.

8
What to Expect in College

It is becoming more and more obvious that it is not starvation, not microbes, not cancer but man himself who is mankind's greatest danger.

(Psychoanalyst Carl G. Jung)

"A little learning can be a dangerous thing," was a maxim I heard occasionally when growing up. It became an adult preachment after some young person had gone halfcocked (not fully prepared) into a project. Having what the old-timers called "head sense but no horse sense," the person often rued his behavior. He discovered that what he did not know could hurt him.

Going to college has been a way many American young people have prepared for adulthood. We have felt that knowledge is power—that one's judgment was no better than his information. Persons who wished to transcend rural beginnings or blue-collar jobs were told to get a higher education. The lure of professional status and income following a college degree, along with the fun, color, and challenges of campus life, has attracted millions of Americans to university campuses.

Not everyone elects to enroll in college or professional school. We have discovered that skilled craftsmen may earn potentially as much as a college professor in a lifetime, that plumbers may be wealthier than physicians, and that many self-made millionaires never finished a university. On the other hand, college has become the key to effective living for countless youths—male, female, white, and black. In fact, America's great, wealthy universities draw students from across the world. These learning factories have budgets of tens of millions of dollars, attract scholars in specialized fields of research, and are melting pots of international culture.

Let's assume that you will go to college at least one year. What should you expect?

Looking Ahead

How can you get a clear picture of what is happening on the American university campus? Looking at public relations materials about athletic victories and campus life? Spending a "roundup" weekend in a fraternity sponsored sex party? Looking at a current catalog of courses? Hearing students gripe about conservative administrators and stupid professors? Visiting a campus, attending classes, meeting varied teachers and students, and discovering facts for yourself?

The last idea is your best chance since each campus is unique. There is no such thing as *the* campus mood, despite attempts by journalists to create a monolithic image of American college campuses.

America's nearly 2,000 colleges and universities differ in size, location, sponsorship, history, financial support, intellectual climate, student life, and faculty qualifications. While there are parallels, colleges are not identical. A campus, like a person, develops its own identity, style, and traditions. Educational centers are private and public, coeducational and non-coeducational, large and small, informal and traditional, modernistic and Gothic in architecture, sectarian and unrestricted in character.

"A picture . . . of which campus?" one is forced to ask. Imagine the feelings of a freshman student from Tupelo, Mississippi, seeing the stately quadrangles of an Ivy League university for the first time. Put a young New Yorker on a conservative campus, and restrictions seem like reform school.

How can you, feeling so up-in-the-air about many things,

speak realistically about college? Motivation can't be dumped in someone else's lap. Here are questions that a teenager thinking about college should answer.

Am I college material? What if I got into some school, then flunked out? Who wants to be a failure before twenty? One's IQ (intelligence quotient) can be measured in a written or an oral test, administered by a competent counselor. But an IQ score does not measure ability accurately in all cases. One might score well above average, say 138, be a wizard in English, yet fail trigonometry.

It's smart to check your abilities and achievements with your teachers or guidance department counselor each year. During your junior year take the preliminary scholastic aptitude test administered through nationally recognized agencies like the College Entrance Examination Board and American College Testing Program. Test results will give you some idea of national test score norms, and guide you toward an academic program meeting college requirements. You may not win a National Merit scholarship, nor graduate Phi Beta Kappa from college, but it's wise to want a good education. Be willing to work for it.

How do colleges select students? Can I be admitted with just average test scores? Are college admissions officers interested in people or test scores or both? Admissions criteria differ in private and state universities. Politics still influence some admission committee members' decisions.

Colleges select students on several bases: one's high school record, test scores, personality, achievements in and outside school, and letters of recommendation from significant adults. State schools, because of their tax-based support, screen candidates liberally. A student who is not ready for college work, however, may be placed on probation or suspended for poor academic performance.

It is important to plan ahead if you expect to attend college. Getting admitted is a process of planning and pursuing one's goal years in advance.

Getting Admitted

Which school for you? Where will you apply for admission—in one, two, or a half-dozen good schools? That all depends. "On what?" you wonder. On factors like:

1. Requirements for admission in a specific school;
2. Advantages and disadvantages of living at home and attending a commuter college;
3. What college costs (Anywhere from $2,500 to $10,000 a year, depending on the school you select);
4. Scholarships—academic, athletic, and other aid which might be available;
5. Learning resources—faculty strength, library tools, research facilities, cooperative ties with other campuses;
6. Pressures from parents, teachers, friends, and alumni;
7. Basic orientation—religious or secular, liberal arts or science, military or civilian, prestige or small, etc.;
8. Vocational goals and job opportunities upon graduation.

There is a right college for you, though it may not be a prestige school or the same university your parents attended.

For admission, follow application procedures listed in your school catalog. Send proper fees, health certificate, room application, test scores, school records, and so on. If you apply at several schools and are accepted at all of them, notify those you do not plan to attend.

Orientation sessions for new students and interested parents are usually offered during the summer months and at the start of each semester. Many questions can be answered, fears resolved, and problems avoided by determining school policies and procedures during orientation.

Coping with Campus Life

You may have seen the cartoon of a first-grade pupil, standing beside his mother, "talking" with his father who was reading the daily paper. Without looking up, the man said: "Now, your daddy won't have time to listen to what happens to you every day at school, but he definitely wants a report, a summation, if you will, when you get your college degree." One wonders if we understand growth processes at all.

In American culture, the college experience is valued as an opportunity for you to learn new social roles and skills that will prepare you for adult responsibilities. A campus—elite, prestige, or plain—offers a novel and problematic environment for growth. Your informational horizon expands, true enough, yet meaningful growth involves the entire ego. Growing up, as Marshall McLuhan says, is *total.*

How can one explain the elating—depressing ups and downs of the college world to someone who hasn't been around a university campus? It's not easy, but I can try.[21]

Students must cope successfully with six tasks in order to (1) meet social expectations, (2) maintain self-esteem and develop a sense of worth, and (3) manage emotional distress in the face of complex demands at college. These tasks include:

Learning new academic skills and competencies. One girl said: "They require more work but it is more exciting and interesting than in high school." Let's imagine the experience of a biology student (one who misunderstood in high school Charles Darwin's long argument, *The Origin of Species by Means of Natural Selection*) upon reading in his text:

> The theory of evolution is quite rightly called the greatest unifying theory in biology. The diversity of organisms, similarities and differences between kinds of organisms, patterns of distribution and behavior, adaptation and interaction, all this was merely a bewildering chaos of facts until given meaning by the evolutionary theory. There is no area in biology in which that theory has not served as an ordering principle.[22]

Reared in a conservative religious atmosphere, where divine creation by fiat was accepted unquestioningly, he may fail to distinguish theory from fact. Whose authority can he accept—God's word, his parents', or the textbook's view?

Tell this freshman that he can go *beyond* Darwin's study, since nineteenth-century man had no access to the electron microscope which aids investigation and interpretation of cellular substructures. Darwin had no basis, for example, for understanding the complex chemistry of heredity—DNA and RNA. The mystery deepens when he studies human ecology and discovers that modern evolutionary notions go beyond Darwin to the manipulation and management of human life and death. Tomorrow's student faces questions about test-tube babies and creation of life, synthetic genes that may correct genetic defects, mind-bending and behavior-modifying drugs, and population control through euthanasia. Exploding fields of knowledge—from avionics to ekistics—require mastery.

Developing close and meaningful friendships, as well as productive work relations, with one's peers. Moving to a college campus permits the freshman to start with a clean slate of friends. He or she can try new relationships "on for size," pool information through informal group discussions, and clarify expectations by using upperclassmen as a sounding board for varied views.

Friendships are formed generally in two stages. Initially, one warms up and reaches out to almost any one who accepts him. It is imperative to overcome loneliness and to identify with others who are "in the same boat" when everything is new and confusing. Physical proximity—one's roommate or dormitory neighbor—usually affects first acquaintances.

Later, though one knows many people in classes, and so on, he develops deeper relationships with a few significant persons whom he calls friends. Such ties are based on shared interests and values with a member of one's own or the opposite sex. Strivings for intimacy and identity flow together.

Dealing with physical separation from one's family, and regulating one's need for autonomy and relatedness to one's parents. When one is deeply attached to parents and home, leaving the first time for college floods him with mixed emotions. There is the freedom of being on one's own, away from mother's apron strings, delicious meals, and father's protective advice. Yet there is still the deeply felt need for economic and emotional security registered by a freshman girl: "Being here, away from home, it's up to me to decide how high I want to fly. Knowing there's still a net to catch me if I fall reassures me of many things—that net being my parents."

If one discovers that, in Thomas Wolfe's memorable phrase, he "can't go home again," where shall he turn for guidance, sympathy, value reinforcement, and affection? Likely, he will turn to friends, dates, and persons from different regional and cultural backgrounds who enrich his value system. A favorite faculty member may become an identification model. The growing student incorporates attitudes, traits (even bothersome ones), and ways of relating which he learns from others.

A fourth task is self-regulation in organizing time and activity. Campus life demands individual initiative and organizing ability in duties as varied as learning chemistry formulas, attending chapel (in private schools), and washing soiled laundry. Pressures on a student's time are incredible.

You will soon discover that wasting time and procrastination are two common "sins" on campus. "Why do today what you can put off until tomorrow?" your "roomie" reasons. "Next week," quipped one crummy character to another in a cartoon picturing sloppiness, "we're gonna have to get organized." Have you ever felt like that?

A student enduring his first experience away from home described his depressing confusion: "It's like facing a wall one thousand miles long. Doors are everywhere, but I don't know which ones to enter and which ones to avoid."

A coed described herself as a "home-type person with a big adjustment to make" as one of 19,000 students on a state university campus.

So, how does a student survive? Through trial and error, following reliable guidance, you discipline yourself in the light of new freedoms. Watch your own calendar and clock. Keep up with your checkbook and bank balance. You may feel like goofing off when there's studying to be done. With freer regulations of collegiate life, it's up to you to put first things first. Else who will come to your rescue?

Pairing off through dates, achieving intimacy with a cherished person of the opposite sex, and preparing for marriage. Sex makes the collegiate world go 'round. Guys speak endearingly of the campus student center as "the body shop." Girl-watching becomes an ingenious hobby. Matchmaking abounds. One freshman coed reported a dating experience that turned sour. "Harry—this guy I just met this fall—asked me out to 'dinner,' then took me to Raco's Taco Drive-in. You know how messy tacos are, rolled up, and dripping. Then he drove to the darkest part of a large park and stopped. Wow! Was I scared!"

All of which says—keep your head on and your brains working. College sex is no light matter. True, many collegians pursue extracurricular sex games, but living together is a far cry from composer John Howard Payne's *Home Sweet Home.*

Handling conflicts of opinion between students, faculty, and the administration. Coming to terms with authority provokes some of youth's most dramatic, intense struggles. At home, the individual runs into varied adult reactions—indifference, domination, fraternizing, scapegoating, even outright rejection. One high school senior, Kathryn Ann, said that she was just "living to get away from home." You may know some individual who "waited out" high school in order to gain his or her independence.

Adults, however, often have the last laugh. Most of them have lived long enough to discover how illusory freedom can be. There is enough of your parents in you, because of early identification and later positive and negative modeling, so that your "independence" actually grows out of early experiences in most later relationships. This explains your delight with certain faculty members and anxiety in the presence of others. For some (unconscious) reason, you dislike a pushy professor who reminds you of an aggressive parent or you identify with a profane person who "tells off" authority figures in his lectures. In rejecting the existing moral, social, or political order, he speaks *for* you.

Someone once said, "Anybody who gets out of college having had his confidence in the perfection of existing institutions affirmed has not been educated—just suffocated." Education stretches us toward new horizons, new dreams, and new possibilities. Ideally, it prepares one for adult tasks like those addressed in chapter 9.

9
Steps Toward Adulthood

Who wants to be a millionaire? I don't.
Have flashy flunkeys ev'rywhere? I don't.
Who wants to ride behind a liv'ried chauffeur?
Do I want? No sir!

(Composer Cole Porter, 1955)

By now, you have spent quite a bit of time reading this book. The picture of a journey has persisted in each discussion. You are leaving childhood and mid-adolescence in order to arrive at a place called adulthood. When you arrive, you'll discover that adulthood is more of a process than a place.

You'll cry for help along the way, for, in fairness, it's a critical pilgrimage. And you are not alone. Four billion plus passengers share your ride on spaceship earth. Don't be ashamed to ask the way from people who should know. Many of your fellow pilgrims are farther along the pathway than yourself. We need your dreams, vitality, comedy, and optimism as much as you need our consultation, caution, comfort, and companionship.

While you may be only thirteen or sixteen, any steps you take toward adulthood matter. Decisions about your vocation, money, and marriage lie ahead. Since you're interested in working, always need money, and live in some type of family arrangement, these subjects should appeal to you.

Vocation

Whether one becomes a blue- or white-collar worker; is self-employed or owns a business; receives a salary, fees, dividends from investments, or an hourly wage; is skilled, unskilled, or semiskilled, in the final analysis are vocational decisions. In the course of a lifetime some persons do all these things and more!

One's work involves one's abilities, experiences, preferences, opportunities, failures, and achievements. Tastes as well as commitments are involved. Certain needs—like recognition, service, esteem, and money—influence what you do with your life, along with your understanding of God's will. Some would say one's career is primarily a matter of luck or breaks. Jobs like political office, on the other hand, must be sought and won through the confidence of an electorate.

Where Do I Fit In? One worker prefers jeans, boots, a hard hat, lunch pail, special skill, and regular hours. Another prefers a professional life-style, with advanced education, well-groomed appearance, cultured clients, and country club social circles. Another prefers the push and power of an executive's deals. One person's idea of success fails to appeal to another individual. Travel is a tonic for some workers. Trips, like commuting, tire other people. Decision making exhilarates some persons and exhausts others.

One's vocation is his or her calling in life. Whether the work is God's will or human choice is subject to interpretation. Some young people enter vocations through ability testing, satisfying achievements, and financial rewards.[23] Others seek prayerfully to determine God's purpose for their lives, then enter a calling in deeply religious terms. That certainly should be true for ministers and all vocational Christian workers. Many laymen feel called as well.

The Bible is filled with experiences of men and women who responded to God's touch in their lives and followed his plan. Old Testament stories feature men like Abraham, Jacob, Joseph, Samson, Samuel, David; and women like Esther, Sarah (wife of Abraham), Hannah (mother of the prophet Samuel), and Bathsheba (wife of David). The New Testament tells how disciples obeyed Christ's call to become "fishers of men." Saul—later Paul the apostle—obeyed his Master's voice following conversion. Men like Matthew, Mark, Luke, and John recorded God's holy Word. God is pictured as making a difference in the lives of women like Elizabeth, mother of John the Baptist; Mary, the mother of Jesus Christ; and Lydia, a seller of purple in Philippi who befriended the apostle Paul. Discovering what should be done with their lives was more than a matter of life-style, however; it involved obedience.

The world of work is changing constantly. Meaningful work and play are essential to any individual's sense of well-being. You deserve the dignity and earnings of creative effort.

A Time of Opportunity. Young people frequently begin careers with part-time and summer job experiences. Without the seriousness of "playing for keeps," you can earn money, test likes and dislikes, and risk yourself in contacts with other persons. At the end of the holiday period or summer vacation, you head back to school usually wiser, and maybe wealthier, for your experiences. Given national legislation for a minimum wage and fair employment practices, boys and girls are remunerated equally well for their first efforts at jobs.

Possessions that income provide bring you self-esteem and status with your friends—a stereo set, camera, clothes, or a new car, for example. Things can also compensate for psychological insecurity. One accumulates records, jewelry, recreational vehicles, and other cherished status symbols in an effort to prove: "I am worthy. If you cannot accept me for what I *am*, recognize me for what I *possess*."

I once talked with a vocational arts teacher about a steel chisel my son had forged in metal craft class. "A lot of work went into forging and grinding that piece of steel."

"Yes," he replied, "but what happened to the boy who shaped the steel is more important than the chisel itself." Here was a piece of work he had done. Such creative efforts fortify one's sense of worth. You, not just materials, are valuable. Art and hobbies, products made as crafts by hand as well as athletic achievements, build esteem and prepare one for work.

Caution. Everyone isn't healthy and ambitious. Mentally retarded and physically handicapped young people must depend upon parents and other sources of help. They are subject to more frustrations than healthy citizens and fight depressing feelings of differentness. With development of aptitudes and skills some of them can be wholly or partially self-supporting. It takes courage to occupy a wheelchair.

A discussion of work leads naturally to the subject of money —that which one receives in payment for labor or service rendered. Learning to manage money is crucial in growing up.

Money

I have known people with money and without money, each of whom was miserable. Financial resources are no guarantee of happiness. Ambitious fat cats—with big incomes, sprawling estates, and great power—may support an army of lawyers and psychiatrists! Like the poor, the rich are often in trouble. There are now more than half a million millionaires in the United States, according to the U.S. Trust, a New York firm that specializes in handling other people's money.

Probably you will work for a salary or fees, like many fellow Americans, but you could be wealthy someday.

Understanding Money. Money has served mankind for centuries as a measure of value and medium of exchange. Bartering was early man's easiest means of getting something he wanted in exchange for something he possessed. Sheep, perhaps, were traded for grain. Early American settlers in the Eastern colonies traded manufactured products, like knives and guns, to the Indians in exchange for furs and tobacco.

Later, coins of gold, silver, and copper were stamped and exchanged in the purchase of land, goods, and services. The North American Indians used wampum (beads made of shells) as money, ceremonial pledges, and ornaments. South American Indians used precious stones, like emeralds in Columbia and tourmalines in Brazil, as money.

With the advent of the industrial revolution came factory

workers who wished to be paid in coins or paper certificates of current monetary value (often backed by silver or gold). They had talents and time to give in exchange for paid employment. In the Western United States, gold dust was used as money in the nineteenth century. While bartering continues worldwide to the present day, money or monetary credit is the universal medium of exchange.

Money has long been tied to one's ego, sense of worth, and feeling of power. Ancient kings were noted for their wealth—jewels, lands, castles, herds, and things gold and silver could buy. Merchant princes, who were international traders, rivaled kings and queens in wealth. The Roman Catholic Church acquired much land and improved property—all tax-exempt. People gave offerings voluntarily to priests, but church officials also exacted extravagant contributions from wealthy patrons. For the ordinary worker and fee-taking professional person, money symbolized his skill, time investment, in fact, his life. This was also true of artists, teachers, and artisans.

In addition to tangible assets, like oil and gold, our modern world economy moves on credit, paper transactions, and promises to pay. The billion dollar credit card business, ordinary charge accounts, plus easy bank loans have opened credit operations to almost everyone. Some entrepreneurs have established themselves by creating a line of credit with major financial institutions, acquiring equity in or control of successful corporations, and selling shares of stock. Buying-in and selling-out brought some investors quick wealth, while others lost everything.

Money, then, has been a measure of value, medium of exchange, and extension of the human ego. A person *was* what he or she did and possessed. Poor people, traditionally, have been powerless, but they also have become revolutionaries. Witness the French Revolution! You may know someone who has inherited a fortune and the status accompanying it. As a supreme ego trip, some wheeler-dealers have pursued wealth for fun and profit. Fortunes have been made and lost, mostly on paper, overnight. Money can become one's servant or master in the elusive pursuit of fame and fortune. It has cost many a man his life.

The Bible and Money. Issues like achievement and accountability lead us to ask what the Bible says about possessions.

God's Word has much to say about money (wealth)—its acquisition, management, and disposition. God as creator is pictured in Genesis as sovereign of the universe. He is concerned about every aspect of man's life. Later, when Israel was gathered as a nation, society's welfare was taken into account. Moses taught the covenant people, "You shall remember the Lord your God, for it is He who is giving you power to make wealth, that He may confirm His covenant which He swore to your fathers" (Deut. 8:18, NASB). The principle of stewardship was stamped into the tapestry of a nation's life.

What does the word *steward* mean? In biblical times, a steward was the manager of a large house or estate. Joseph, Jacob's favorite son who was sold into slavery, became a steward in Potiphar's house. Later, he became ruler of Egypt, second in command only to Pharaoh (Gen. 38—50). Old Testament persons were taught: "Honor the Lord from your wealth," since possessions were a sign of divine favor (Prov. 3:9, NASB). All God's people were stewards and were to pay a tenth (tithe) part of their produce or income for his work (Lev. 27:30; Num. 18:26-28; Matt. 23:23; Luke 11:42). The tithe symbolized all their possessions as sacred to God.

Moving beyond fear of punishment and obedience to duty, love and generosity motivated Christ's followers to care (2 Cor. 8:2). The apostle Paul interpreted stewardship in the widest possible terms and applied it to all of life. "I have a stewardship entrusted to me," he wrote, as a "steward(s) of the mysteries of God" (1 Cor. 4:1, 9:17, NASB). This "stewardship of

God's grace" is something each of us can feel and express (Eph. 3:2, NASB).

Crucial to biblical understanding of economics is what any practice or system does to persons. This is because of God's concern for human personality. People who profit greedily at others' expense or take advantage of the poor are in danger of divine judgment. (See the book of Amos.) The ultimate test of our capitalistic system, as well as of Communism, is not its technological achievements or sophisticated weapons but the quality of life it produces. Great power involves great responsibility. That principle is true whether power is measured in resources like oil and gold or abilities like modern technology and health care.

Getting What You Want. Some laws of life seem inexorable. One of them is that, usually, you get what you go after. There are exceptions of course. Given good health and the opportunity to pursue goals, you will likely achieve your objectives. Worldlings devote themselves to success in this life, whether achievement is measured in possessions, professional achievements, or recognition. Christians take a longer look at reality—at God's law of spiritual harvest (Gal. 6:7).

The Bible is clear. Each one of us shall give an account of himself to God. One who has prized the kingdom of God—loved the heavenly Father and pursued his purpose—will find that "things shall be added," as Christ said (Matt. 6:33). Jesus did not minimize money. Rather, he taught the principle of priority. Possessions, things, wealth are of secondary consequence. Money is never to be sought as an end in itself (Matt. 6:24-34). We are to guard against greed. After all, Jesus warned, "What shall a man give in exchange for his soul?" (Mark 8:37).

Given our temporariness on this planet and accountability to God, what do you want? You must decide how much of this world's wealth you'll go after in one lifetime. You will have some money to spend, first as an allowance from your parents, later from your own earnings. When you work, give an honest day's service for an honest day's pay. Save or invest part of your earnings, not merely for emergencies, but for vacations, travel, fun things, even small luxuries you might enjoy. Be generous toward God, the church, and with other people. In addition, support government officials who honor God and respect human personality.

My hunch is that you will be a wholesome creator of wealth and consumer of goods. Shortages of natural resources, like oil, and runaway inflation will press members of your generation to fresh creativity. Books are published regularly to help you understand money and survive in the marketplace.[24] Newspapers, like *The Wall Street Journal,* and magazines, like *Money,* advise Americans of changes happening in the economy. You will profit, in time, from courses in economics and seminars led by bankers or investment counselors. Carefully selected attorneys, accountants, and trust officers of savings institutions may be relied upon for wise counsel.

You may not become a financial expert. As a normal, money-conscious citizen, please act on the best advice you can get. You are wise to feel concerned about your long-range financial health and that of your country.

We have examined the world of work and matter of money. The last step toward adulthood considered here is marriage.

Marriage

Sex urges are seldom more powerful among men and appealing among women than in late adolescence, traditionally a period of singleness in the United States. Just because youths remain single does not imply, however, that they remain sexually inactive. Authorities tell us that "an estimated 4.2 million girls aged fifteen to nineteen are sexually active. Yet only 30 percent of them claim to use an effective contraceptive, and more than a quarter admit to using none at all."[25] Small wonder that six hundred thousand babies were born to unwed mothers under twenty in one recent year. Many teens rush into sexual relationships before they are ready to deal with the consequences.

People have for centuries lived together without benefit of formal marriage rites. Viewed as living "in sin," many such couples remained together in common-law marriages. Now, the children of such live-in arrangements are partly protected under the law.

Your generation faces a speedup in the numbers of couples "living together," as well as in the results (such as children) of such arrangements. The Census Bureau discovered more than one million unmarried male-female couples living together in a recent survey. Such illicit arrangements have more than doubled in less than a decade. Part of the explanation is a desire to avoid the perils of divorce while enjoying the privileges of sexual union. Demographers attributed the trend to "an increasing desire among young adults to pursue nonfamilial interests."[26] The sharpest rise has occurred among couples in the under twenty-five category.

Many young people prefer singleness to the risks of an unhappy marital relationship. Eighteen percent of women between twenty-five and twenty-nine are single, many by choice. One reason is that divorce is now so common, said the Census Bureau report, that the number of families headed by a woman has climbed to eight million. Whether we call it single parenting or a broken home, the stresses and strains of work, finances, child care, meal planning and preparation, home management, laundry, shopping, and rearing offspring are enormous. Shockingly, almost half of all children born today can expect to spend a portion of their lives before age eighteen in single-parent families. It is difficult to imagine what psychological effects that may have on the young.

So, the matter of marriage today is much more complicated than selecting the length of one's bridal veil and number of bridesmaids in the wedding party.

Marriage involves finding a partner who will not cross his or her fingers when vowing to love "'til death do us part." It takes companions who will blend their desires for meaningful occupations and homelife, who will commit themselves to life together under God. Most young women must work in order to supplement family income or to support a husband who may still be in school. Stresses and strains cannot be avoided in such dual-career marriages.

The time has come for couples to prize marriage vows, cherish each other "for better or worse," care for their offspring, and remain faithful to each other (no matter what comes). People have all sorts of convenient excuses for not staying married these days. The place to avoid flippancy lies at the gateway to marriage—God's good gift—rather than bidding one's mate good-bye after a small spat.

Someone may be really important in your life right now. Before you marry, think about the answer to these questions. (1) Have I finished school? (2) Can I provide financially for a mate or family? (3) Am I reasonably independent of my parents? (4) Have I dated enough to know definitely the right person for me? (5) Am I ready to settle down and live with the one I love? If you answered "yes" to these questions, you may be mature enough for marriage.

We have been attracted to work, money, and marriage as big steps toward adulthood. This discussion will not guarantee your employment, wealth, or marital happiness. It does dispel some myths and provide positive guidance. Successful living to you!

10
Facing the Drug Dilemma

> The electric rim-spin on our planet is much beyond the adaptive power of the human population. The overall speedup of transactions creates vast depression of body and spirit alike. Drugs may seem to offer a means of achieving the necessary "speed." In fact, however, a great psychic depression has occurred.
>
> (Educator Marshall McLuhan, 1970)

"Should a person's future be ruined by one 'trip' or experience of smoking 'pot'?" asked seventeen-year-old Ricky. He is not on drugs but knows some teenagers who use them.

To raise such a question is part of youth's curiosity, but the subject of drugs arouses a hornet's nest of controversy. Observers say Ricky's question multiplies issues, all subject to dispute: Is marijuana a drug of "psychic dependence"? Does it cause "psychotic episodes" (make you crazy) or damage one's brain? How does marijuana influence motor skills, like driving an automobile, and artistic creativity? Answers are biased, according to one's conservative-liberal style of life.

Many parents of teenagers do not sleep well. Besides the traditional fears of drinking, reckless driving, premarital sex, religious cults, and sudden death at the hands of a mad gunman, there is now the narcotics nightmare. Because of its illegal status and unknown side effects, parents try to influence youth away from marijuana.

Recent evidence indicates that marijuana use is increasing in the United States. It is estimated that more than half of the eighteen to twenty-five year age group have tried marijuana and that one-third of all college students in the country are current users.[27] Younger and younger teenagers, along with eleven- and twelve-year-olds, are inhaling, swallowing, and injecting an astonishing array of chemical substances. Studies indicate that vast numbers of youth die of heroin overdoses each year. Cocaine has now replaced LSD and other narcotics at parties in middle-class homes. Forty-four million prescriptions for Valium were written in the United States last year.

Talking or Taking?

The allure of drugs, including beer and hard liquor, is compelling. "Sure, I turn on every two or three weeks. I've never had any trouble when I turn on. It makes me feel good in an excited-all-over sort of way. I like to be around people when I'm high. I laugh, enjoy people, and accept them as they are. My friends can tell when I'm high. They enjoy my company as much then as at other times."

This description of some effects of marijuana comes from a minister's son, with a solid B standing, who is not angry with his parents. He looks clean-cut, yet has been persuaded by his peer reference group to smoke pot.[28]

Some teenagers take, others talk, about the mind-benders. Many experiment once or twice and quit. Others continue and get hooked. The surge of student suicides—blamed on low self-esteem, alienation, poor grades, religious cult involvement, psychic confusion, and sexual problems—may be linked, in part, to the predicament of drug dependency.

"Forbidden fruit is always the sweetest," goes the old adage. There is a magnetism, a mysterious appeal, of drugs on the teenage scene. You hear rumors of a weekend pot party at a friend's lake cabin while her parents were in Denver on a business trip. Somebody who hasn't used drugs turns on once, then reports a delightful sensation. Damage appears minor, feelings appear happier, until the daughter of a former television celebrity like Art Linkletter leaps to her death, until her father explains that she could not cope with reality as a teenage divorcee and was on LSD.

You know the quaint vocabulary kids sling around. They talk about drugs as much to frighten, at least irritate, their elders as anything. You may be curious about drug talk.

The amphetamines or stimulants are known as "Bennies, Crystals, Co-Pilots, Dexies, Drivers, Footballs, Hearts, Oranges, Peaches, Pep Pills, Reds, Roses, and Wake Ups." The barbiturates or sedatives are known as "Blue Heavens, Candy, Devils, Double Trouble, Downs, Peanuts, Phennies, Purple Hearts, Red Devils, and Yellow Jackets."

LSD (lysergic acid diethylamide), the consciousness expanding psychedelic which promises instant paradise, is also called "Acid, Big D., Chief, Cubes, Hawk, Sugar, and Trips." Angel Dust, popular in some drug circles, is as lethal as LSD. Marijuana, a milder hallucinogen, is actually a depressant, affecting one's body like alcohol. It is also known as "Gage, Grass, Hay, Hemp, Jive, Mary Jane, Mezz, MU, Muggles, Pot, Rope, Tea, and Weed." Marijuana cigarettes are called "Joints, Sticks, or Reefers." High-grade marijuana is called "Manicure." The addictive drug heroin, an opiate, is referred to as "Dope, Hard Stuff, Harry, H., Horse, Junk, Scat, Smack, and Snow." So goes the jargon, and it changes.

The fifteen-year-old daughter of an engineer came home from high school one day with this report: "Some girls were in the rest room today spraying hair spray into paper bags; then they were getting high inhaling the stuff." My! Was her mother ever upset by that scary tale.

To get high, some kids will try almost anything. They swallow pills, sniff glue, inhale fumes, and gulp cough syrup. They are blind to any danger and deaf to grown-up's warnings. "We want to live today; tomorrow may never come," is the going argument. It sends parents into spasms.

"Why do they desire stuff like that?" you wonder. "Why do kids get mixed up with drugs, live a day-to-day existence, steal, shoplift, or sell dope in order to buy drugs themselves?"

A twenty-one-year-old plainclothesman grew a beard, joined a colony of junkies in a city park, and reported his undercover findings. "They want anything that will give them a buzz. If they can't get what you might call 'regular drugs,' they'll shoot anything—Dristan, cough medicine or anything with a drug label on it. There was one guy who loved the needle. I've watched him shoot up with heroin and he'd shoot a little bit and then pull the needle out of his arm. He'd wait awhile and shoot some more. He loved that needle. He would stick it in and out of his arm.

"Then there were the little twelve- and thirteen-year-old girls who would come down to the park because they thought it was cool and the people they met there were 'free.' Really, they were all mad at their parents. Some were too lax and some were too strict."

What's Behind Drug Involvement?

There's a lot of misinformation going around about drug use and abuse. Some journalists prefer sensationalism, make the "hard stuff" appear cool, and the addict a culture hero to juveniles. Movies, picturing ecstasy and power, and avoiding the terror and temporary psychotic episodes induced by hallucinogens, demoralize rather than help young people to cope intelligently with chemical crutches.

An Albuquerque housewife reported the dangers of miseducation among parents, teachers, and concerned youth. She warned against confusing advice. "We attended a PTA meeting on drug abuse that tended to confuse all drugs with heroin; refused to include alcohol as a dangerous drug; thrilled over endless, sensational anti-kid stories; pictured a pusher as a bearded fellow with rolling eyes; emphasized detection techniques—going through drawers, testing eyes; advised frightening the kids and showing authority."

You need to check the source of your data thoroughly. Thoughtful persons are giving their lives in the study and prevention of drug abuse. Others offer a hoax, witchcraft, and bad news that worries but fails to inform intelligent citizens. "Who says?" is a better response than "You don't say!" Skepticism should lead cautious teenagers, not to escapism, but to discover the truth. Since drugs offer a shaky ship for life's uncertain voyage, why do kids get high?

One man who has made a lengthy study of this problem is UCLA psychiatrist J. Thomas Ungerleider, M.D. He cited seven reasons for youth's involvement.[29]

Curiosity about drugs, engendered by our adult drug culture—including tobacco (nicotine), coffee (caffeine), alcohol, tranquilizers, diet pills, sleeping pills, and pep pills—advertised everywhere.

Peer group pressure. It is almost becoming a puberty rite to have experimented with drugs by the time you are fourteen or fifteen. It is one of the most talked about subjects today.

Affluence and permissiveness. Bored teenagers with a car, money, and no responsibilities or meaningful work opportunities have plenty of opportunity to experiment with alcohol and drugs.

Rebelliousness. Kids see drugs as a way to get their parents or teachers uptight, frightened, or anxious.

Instant acceptability. Kids think they can create an identity by getting involved in the drug scene; it's easier than long hours of study, band rehearsals, or athletic practice.

Psychedelics such as marijuana and LSD can *dampen internal conflicts and insecurities* (and prevent coming to grips with them) without losing consciousness, as one does with sleeping pills or too much alcohol. But it is the very struggle with these feelings that leads to maturity and emotional growth.

Finally, some young people use drugs *just "for kicks."*

Opinions vary as to physical effects of these drugs. LSD "does not seem either to stimulate or diminish sexual drive," says one medical report. There is some evidence that it may damage human chromosomes. Teenage users risk birth defects in their offspring. One study showed that chronic marijuana users get the same high smoking joints lacking the actual "grass" ingredient as they did with real marijuana. Thus, some perceptions and distortions are self-induced. A teenager who enjoys life may experience a good trip. If you're depressed and smoke pot, you're likely to get more depressed. A suicidal student gets more suicidal. Such news cannot be viewed lightly. Your life is at stake.

"Can kids who've tried it quit or is there no place to go once you've started turning on?" Some students who had tried marijuana and LSD answered in an anonymous questionnaire.

"I have stopped taking drugs. It became too easy to 'groove' on something . . . without ever coming to terms with real problems, without ever really thinking. The borders of illusion and reality became hazy."

An older adolescent wrote: "I consider it now a part of the growing up process. It was an answer. It no longer is. I am still overwhelmed by the madness that is my country, but I must find another way of coming to terms with it."

You probably have friends who are smoking marijuana and haven't flipped out or are still making good grades. You may be tempted to try it yourself. Before seeking escape in drugs, consider the possible emptiness after the party's over. Here are some things you should know about alcohol and drug abuse.

Perspectives on a Complex Problem

In your town, on your campus, the drug problem may be small. But, in some schools, a high percentage of students have experimented with drugs, including alcohol. The general public dreads the hard-core user, arrests, and prosecutes (when possible) professional drug pushers.

A bunch of guys and gals you know may have tried it. You alone can't stamp out marijuana or alcohol, but you can try to deal intelligently with it when it comes your way. Here are three perspectives on drugs to help you face street corner myths.

Medical.—Stanley Yolles, M.D., former director, National Institute of Mental Health, answers teen questions.[30] To quote:

Is it safe to try drugs once just to see how it feels?

This depends entirely upon the drug and the person—both of which involve important unknown quantities. Few people who try heroin once, for example, never touch it again. On the other hand, a majority of people who try marijuana do so fewer than ten times before quitting entirely.

Can I become addicted to "pot"?

Marijuana does not cause addiction. But it can be as habit-forming as ordinary cigarettes. Chronic users become dependent upon it psychologically. Without it, they may feel restless, unable to face life.

What should I do at a party where everyone is on drugs and they're trying to get me to take them?

Leave immediately! Most people start on drugs the first time in just such circumstances. Even if you stay but don't "turn on," you are in danger legally. A person present where drugs are being used can be arrested along with the users.

Isn't marijuana safer than alcohol?

We have much yet to learn about the long-range effects of marijuana. Both intoxicants can impair your physical coordination and hamper your judgment.

Will using "pot" lead to other drugs?

Most occasional marijuana smokers never "progress" to stronger substances. But heavy, regular users (or "potheads") often do. These people are likely to be emotionally disturbed and seem to have a basic need to try other drugs.

What can happen during a "bad trip" on LSD?

Almost anything. The sense of losing control during hallucinations can cause you to panic and blindly injure yourself or others. Because of feelings of omniscience and indestructibility, the "tripper" may believe he can fly and plunge to his death from a high window as many have done.

Is it true that "speed" kills?

Some medical authorities estimate that once you become hooked on "speed" your life expectancy is about five years. Besides the risk of brain damage, habitual use takes a heavy toll on the user's liver and heart.

Can I become addicted to "medicine chest" drugs?

Definitely. In fact, many young people are getting "high" illicitly on the very drugs their parents use under prescription.

Can a person stop using drugs by himself?

Once you are addicted or habituated to drugs, it is very unlikely that you can "cure" yourself. In some cases, deep-seated psychological or character disorders, which require psychiatric treatment, may lie behind drug taking. An abrupt withdrawal from some drugs is dangerous. For these reasons, hospitalization or at least close professional supervision while kicking the drug habit is most desirable.

Legal.—United States legal codes are not uniform concerning drug offenses. In some states pot-smoking might bring only misdemeanor charges. State statutes classify drug offenses in two categories—possession and sale. First offense possession of a drug may be taken lightly, but conviction and punishment for its sale might involve several years in prison. A local attorney can provide information about laws in your particular state.

Personal.—In my judgment, some things are best never begun. "Drugs for kicks" is one of those things you can avoid with profit. There are enough worries over peer acceptance, sex, grades, parents, acne, health, loneliness, alcohol, and tobacco—myriads of other problems—that it's depressing to add drugs to the list.

Curiosity may have already gotten the best of you. Maybe you did not know who to believe. If you're already hooked and want to stop, where do you go for help? Read a book on the weed of death, run away to Mexico, kill yourself? Hardly!

Turn to someone you trust—a teacher, parent, doctor, or friend—and ask that person to help you locate the best professional help available in your community or area of the state. Mixed-up feelings may have turned you to alcohol or drugs in the first place. You cannot unmix them alone. The cure rate for alcohol and drug abusers is discouraging—another good reason not to get involved.

"No" is your final freedom. Use it when you need to. The life you save may be your own.

11
When Things Get You Down

Plan now for the future in case there is one.

(Sign in a New York shop window)

"I wonder if I'm ever going to make my goal because there are so many hells around me." The attractive seventeen-year-old girl who said that was experiencing more than a bad day. She was moody, discouraged, facing frustrations that left her depressed. Her parents were splitting up; she was caving in.

Have you ever wondered, "Why must we go through such a baffling world in order to get to heaven?" If so, you're more human than otherwise. It's a common question.

Lucy, of the famed Schulz comic strip *Peanuts,* talked once about life's "ups" and "downs."

LUCY: Sometimes I get discouraged.

CHARLIE BROWN: Well, Lucy, life does have its ups and downs, you know.

LUCY: But why? Why *should* it?! Why can't my life be all *"ups"?* If I want all "ups," why can't I have them? Why can't I just move from one "up" to another "up"? . . . I don't want any "downs"! I just want "ups" and "ups" and "ups"!

CHARLIE BROWN: I can't stand it. . . .

Life, like the weather, is made of extremes. You are either encouraged—eager about some idea or project—or discouraged. You feel great or sick about a biology exam, for which you had studied three hours. You're ready to tackle things or you're ready to give up. Skies are blue, then a teacher "has it in" for you. Suddenly, your best friend moves or there's a big fight at home, and you feel threatened, insecure.

Most people have troubles at least once in a while. Some people have a load of worries that may weigh them down.

Girls seem to experience bigger mood swings—"upper-ups" and "lower-lows"—than boys. Personality patterns point some youths toward activities, sports achievements and work experiences, and others toward more passive reflection. The female tends to be sensitive, preoccupied with relationships, which leads ultimately to the development of "feminine intuition." Guys tend to bump blindly through rough spots; whereas, girls tend to withdraw, perhaps cry, and talk things over with a friend.

A lot of fantasy thinking goes on among all teenagers. Sometimes your imagination (dark thoughts) gets you in trouble.

After a romantic quarrel, a sixteen-year-old girl said: "I find that since I have been unsuccessful in love I no longer want to share love with another person. How can I increase my capacity for love?" Meanwhile, her boyfriend shot basketball goals two or three days after school and felt better. He wasn't as spellbound by their dating encounters as she was.

Trouble hits teenagers, too, not just Washington, D.C., or the Middle East. Some things happen beyond your control.

Crises Beyond Your Control

Did you happen to see a rerun of *2001: A Space Odyssey?* The movie pictures man's coming struggle with machines in the twenty-first century of space exploration. If the film has a hero, it is space: the stars, planets, and unbelievable distances between earth and interstellar matter in the Milky Way.

Man—Machines. You are not responsible for the dramatic struggle between the United States and Russia to place men on far-flung planets. You must survive, however, in a new galactic ecology.

In *2001,* man takes a back seat to technology and its conflicts with alien environments. Picturing man's beginnings, two hordes of gorillas open the "story" by fighting over a waterhole. Almost too quickly, the film leaps to AD 2001 with a spaceship approaching a satellite port. A story emerges within a story as a flight leaves for Jupiter. The crew members take orders from a programmed computer, a genius named Hal. Eventually, there is a struggle. Distrust builds up between a crew member, Dave, and Hal to the point of Dave's unscrewing Hal's memory banks. The computer is reduced to a stuttering idiot; man and machine have been alienated. Have you noticed how many human jobs machines can do? Does it worry you?

Thermonuclear Weapons. After the shocking bombings of Hiroshima, and Nagasaki, Japan, some U.S. physicists wanted to un-invent the A-bomb. You have suppressed feelings about the bomb, but movies like *China Syndrome* and the SALT talks remind you of man's utter helplessness in the grips of atomic destruction.

Political Revolutions. The movement toward a new world is under way. Strange-sounding names of political leaders who have led uprisings—in Iran, the Middle East, Rhodesia, Central America, or South Africa—pop up in the press. United States journalists highlight struggles for freedom in the earth's far corners, and congressmen junket to China, Russia, Cuba, and "hot spots" to keep tabs on Communist inspired uprisings. Rallies and dissent test the stability of our own government system.

Accidents. Accidents can happen so quickly. You say "good-bye" to your mother and dad, join your friends in a car pool for school, then someone runs a *stop* sign!

"I thought the other car was gonna stop, Mom," explained

Bobby. "It was an old man and his wife. We had the right of way, but they just kept comin' and slammed into us."

Your little sister enjoys swinging on the school playground during recess or free play time. One day your sis falls from a swing and has a brain concussion.

If you're normal, you may enjoy sports. Once in a great while, a baseball flies out of reach and through somebody's plate glass door or window. It may be simple—an inexpensive window pane; it may be complex—a costly sliding door replacement. In any case, you need to admit your involvement in the game and bear your share of the expense.

Suffering. An earthquake wipes out a whole village. A ski resort disappears under a snowslide and forty vacationers are killed. A jet liner overshoots a runway, belly lands in a nearby lake, and ninety-three lives are lost. A girl you know gives birth to a child with a critical heart defect. Tens of thousands of Southeast Asians are forced to flee their homes and risk permanent separation from family members because of Communist persecution. A football player makes a stunning tackle, then is carried from the field to face a lifetime as a cripple. Your father goes over to help a neighbor trim trees and suffers a massive heart attack. One could discover a new relationship with God through hurting.

You can't help it if cancer kills the mother of your best friend, if blacks riot in Detroit, if your little brother is a mongoloid child. Some crises are beyond your control. Your attitude toward such things *is* your responsibility. On this other hand, you help some things to go wrong.

What About Your Hang-Ups?

Your biggest problem right now may be an internal crisis, one of your own making. You may be hung-up over a poor attitude toward persons in authority, anger, guilt, or some questionable habit. Let's illustrate.

Authority, Freedom, and Responsibility. Interpersonal

relations make you uniquely you. Not all ties with others are pleasant as you grow up and demand more freedom. Letting go of parents who have provided for your needs for eighteen or more years is only half the problem. They must let go of you, too, if you're free at last. Two staffers with the Young Life organization, James Oraker and Char Meredith, address such issues in *Almost Grown: A Christian Guide for Parents of Teenagers* (Harper & Row, 1979).

"I told my daughter that, when she married, she was on her own; I was through," reflected a middle-aged father. "But I was dead wrong. It was one of the biggest boo-boos of my life." Though Jan was grown and married, she still needed her father and mother as friends and, occasionally, as financial helpers.

As you become your own man or woman, you'll level with parents, school principals, police officers, and other authority figures. You'll learn that life has rules and regulations for all ages of people; that they apply to you. Some matters like car use or later dating privileges must be negotiated. As you show responsibility, more freedom comes. At least it should.

Anger. "I'm so mad at that old bag I could spit!" said Emily on the way home from school one afternoon. "She keeps piling on the algebra homework without grading our papers and telling us the right answers."

Change the setting. You and your sister are talking about a letter she received from Bill at Camp Pendleton. You try to see the message, but she jerks her letter away: "It's none of your business!" For some unexplainable reason, you are madder than mad about her secret love life with Bill.

One other incident. An eighteen-year-old boy is driving the family car on vacation. He gets the wheel from his father after a rest stop and expects to drive a couple of hours until noon. His sister, a sixteen-year-old who recently completed a driver's education course, asks to drive. The pattern goes like this—request, pester, torment, threaten, then attack the older brother. Finally, Joe says, "What do you expect me to do?" And his sister snaps, "You give me a pain in the neck!" Wow!

Hostility happens in the best (as well as the worst) of families. Sometimes, your mother or dad will explode, lash out, misunderstand your motives, or accuse you unjustly. You will be terribly hurt. But what can you do?

Everybody gets mad; you're not the author of *that.* Two points are pivotal: (1) awareness of anger in life situations, and (2) deciding how to use anger. These are both your obligations. Uncontrollable rage is risky. Did you ever see a child throw a temper tantrum—clench his fists and have a "conniption fit"? Automatic anger in a temperamental person racks his whole body. You've seen the symptoms in a high-strung person: the body shakes, face flushes, blood boils, voice quivers. He blows his top, is not like himself, and you flare up protectively in return.

Nature provides us with defenses against attacks. We can deliberately decide what to say or do in a given set of circumstances, or we can fly off the handle. It's wiser to handle a frontal attack—something that makes you mad—with direct, yet careful, conversation than to hit the ceiling. The more in control you are, the healthier your disposition of the hurt.

For example, if you are put out with someone, say: "We're not getting anywhere. Got any clues?"

When parents force teenagers to cap off and bottle upset feelings, they teach the dishonesty of suppression. Sooner or later, anyone who loses face or swallows temper is in trouble. Either physical symptoms like crying, getting a headache, or ulcers occur or revenge takes its deadly toll.

You need to develop healthy ways of coping with everyday, garden variety anger. Holding hatred, like a deep breath, is impossible. One can become temporarily imbalanced and do such risky things as attacking someone physically or with a gun until rage is resolved. Depression, self-punishment for feeling (but not honestly expressing) anger, is hypocrisy's price tag.

The Bible suggests that we are to "speak the truth in love."

This means you need diplomacy, tact, and compassion in order to express anger in nondestructive ways. It's no sin to feel irritated inside, but to hold hatred and seek revenge toward another person is wrong. We all need to learn the power of forgiveness.

Guilt. "Yes, I believe that God can forgive me," said the troubled girl who had spent a weekend fling in a boyfriend's apartment, "but I can't ever forgive myself. I'm ruined." She also feared that her counselor would reject her.

How often have you felt like that? No teenager is loyal to all of his loyalties all of the time. You step over the boundary, even of your self-styled code of ethics, not one imposed by others like dorm or campus rules. The more sensitive your conscience, the greater your suffering and self-punishment when values are violated.

"Americans," said psychiatrist Robert R. Rynearson, "need a value system for all seasons." What does that mean? It suggests:

(1) Relationships are superior to rules in making a go of life. Enduring principles, like love and justice, not codes, support human life.

(2) Relationships may be disrupted by anger, betrayal of trust, absence, indifference, dishonesty, indecency, and violence. Self-centeredness, what the Bible calls pride and psychiatry calls narcissism, is the seedbed of ruined relationships.

(3) Rationalizing by denying guilt-feelings prevents forgiveness. One cannot live well with unresolved feelings of guilt.

(4) Relationships are restored by forgiveness, not by buying back God's or another's love. Once we have accepted another's acceptance of us, we are freed for responsible living again.

Coping with Your Problems

Think it over. You probably have a system figured out for meeting your frustrations. There are healthy and unhealthy ways to escape life's pressures.

I don't know your specific difficulty—not enough money;

your parents distrust you; your sister's too bossy; that special friendship is not working out; hypocrisy with you and those around you. Some problems are little, like having to wash the dishes or mow the front lawn. Some anxieties, like a broken engagement with the person you were to marry, are much greater.

Try to be honest as you answer these questions.

Are you going around looking for trouble? Life at best is risky business. You don't have to look for trouble. It looks for you and will find you. Nobody enjoys a troublemaker.

Have you complied with adult (or legal) precautions? If, for example, your parents have requested that you not travel the 350 miles home from college in a friend's Volkswagen (for safety's sake), did you listen? If you've been cautioned against parking in a high-crime area of the city, did you invite your date home after the late movie? If it is a good idea not to lend a lot of money to other kids, or borrow from them, will conflicts arise if you lend or borrow money?

Do you have a friend or counselor who is trained to help you understand yourself and your problem? There are times when you run into issues or crises that are too big to handle. True, you may want to be alone temporarily, but call for help when you need it. Give your parents or a counselor a chance to try to help you. Most adults will do what they can to help.

Do "bad days" come along once in awhile for everyone? You get a headache. Your stomach hurts. You lose a lot of sleep. You fail a test or don't complete a social studies assignment. Physical feelings can have a big effect on your emotions. Luckily, bad days don't last forever. So this is a bad day! You're cross and irritable. Tomorrow, things will be better.

Can you change, delay, or revise your goal in light of life's realities? Perhaps you want a motorcycle, a new dress, or something that appears impossible. Your parents are against it. You may not have enough money saved for that big purchase. Perhaps you aimed too high—wanted all A's—and have a grade card that looks like a roller coaster, with high and low grades. There is truth in the old adage, "Rome wasn't built in a day." Growing a personality is like erecting a skyscraper—it takes time. Some of our grandest prayers come as we learn to wait.

Have you learned anything from your losses? Troubles have a way of turning around and befriending us to keep us out of more trouble later. Date trouble with one boy can teach you what to avoid next time you're out with a fellow. If blowing up with your dad or a teacher has created "bad news," what will help you control your temper?

Have you forgiven persons who hurt you, and accepted the forgiveness of someone you offended? One of the clues to Jesus Christ's helpful life was his daily living of forgiveness. Rather than worrying about something, or taking yourself too seriously, forget it or work to improve the situation.

Are you releasing pent-up emotions through productive work and relaxing play? Clean up your room, take a hike, listen to music, play tennis. It's amazing what exercise and fun can do.

Problems come to everyone. Some crises are beyond your control. Discovering ways to get on top of your troubles will set the direction of your life. With God's help, you can.

12
Moving Toward Maturity

> Man moves toward health and salvation. . . . Religion says there's always a chance to become creative. There is always something growing in human beings with which you can make an alliance.
>
> (Case conference seminar, psychiatrist Robert S. Glen, M.D.)

A tiny New York harbor tugboat piloted an ocean-going vessel from its berth at dockside to the open sea. The tug's pilot, as a final salute, beamed this message to the ship's captain: "You're on your own now." That is my salute to you.

Throughout these discussions one assumption has run like a golden thread: it's tough growing up. One thing for sure, being a teenager today is no bore. That you are facing life's transitions with courage and candor is a great encouragement to parents like me. Soon, you will be an adult decision maker, on your own. The world will say, "It's up to you now."

I have assumed that you possess the ingredients essential for human growth:

. . . That you inherited a healthy mind and body at birth.

. . . .That you received proper upbringing, plenty of love and sufficient discipline, from your parents.

. . . That you have experienced "normal" life processes and count yourself an average American teenager.

. . . That, if hang-ups (unhealthy emotional patterns) persist you have access to skilled help to correct such problems.

That's quite an assumption—really a compliment to you and your childhood family—since *some* adults remain immature. Hopefully, then, you are the growing kind, and have been freed by responsible adults around you to grow to your full potential.

What Is Maturity?

A young friend asked me: "Is there such a thing as reaching maturity? It seems that life is a process of maturing and that the older adult has not reached full maturity." Do you agree?

Maturity is a term that has been used in various ways. The adjective *mature* comes from the Latin *maturus,* meaning "ripe." In modifying the noun *person, mature* implies a quality, state, or condition of full development. It presupposes a lifelong growth process called maturation. The emerging dynamic self—your own unique personality—grows through several stages. Despite ups and downs, slow periods and fast spurts, you grow as a male or female being.

Yes, all living things—cells, tissues, organisms—are born to grow. Wine, after a fermentation period, is said to reach a desired state of perfection (maturity). Trees push upward in the forest; flowers surge skyward on the mountainside. Animals terminate growth when full physical development comes. Man, unique in all creation, keeps growing in outlook, ideas, hope, and insights until death. The life cycle is then complete.

Growing up is not just physical—marking off notches on grandmother's pantry door to see if you're six feet tall. *Human growth is total, and maturing is a lifelong process.* It includes your social context, economic circumstances, parental willingness both to love and grant you independence, your sexuality, sense of values, life goals, educational opportunities, motives, and grasp of reality.

For our purposes we shall interpret *maturity* to mean the full development of all resources to capacity for a given age. A five-year-old child may be mature if all his or her resources are developed as much as they could be at age five. A seventeen-year-old person is mature, physically and in outlook, if all resources of body, mind, and spirit are developed to full capacity for seventeen years.

You know how boys and girls test themselves to reassure transitions toward adolescence. Boys try physical feats of performance or endurance, like jumping across a creek or jumping across apartment building roofs in the city. Girls play like women by dressing in long frocks and walking in high heels. Both sexes check body development for signs of puberty, like body hair and emerging breasts. Youths also have their own standards for becoming a man or woman. Some teenage growth criteria are appropriate, others unhealthy or unwise. "Proving one's manhood" among some groups can be too risky and costly.

What about immaturity? you wonder. Perhaps you know adults with so many hang-ups from adolescence that they have a terrible time in life. What shall we say of the twenty-year-old who still throws a tantrum like a two-year-old?

No individual develops all his potential resources to full capacity at a given time. Human growth is uneven, not smooth. Different persons develop at different rates and degrees. You, at fifteen, may be lagging behind in mental development while enjoying phenomenal physical growth. Someone you know is way ahead of you socially—already dating, entering talent contests, or performing as an artist in public. You may be shy, feel terribly lonely, yet be his or her age. This difference need not alienate you from the group, but you may have to try a bit harder to be more outgoing with others.

Each age makes its own demands, requires certain tasks be performed, from the cradle to the grave. Maturity at age forty is more demanding than maturity at age eighteen. Still, an eighteen-year-old person faces tremendous challenges in growing up. One needs a healthy, joyous adolescent period as a launchpad into adulthood.

Because growth is always in process, you can speak of maturing (not fully mature) people. Some of your friends are more mature than others. Some cling to selfish baby ways, making excessive demands on adults, too long. The goal of growth is maturity—a healthy, fully-functioning, free, growing person. That's what this book has been about.

Growing Up Free

A common adolescent complaint is:"What gives parents and teachers the idea that pressuring a young person will help him 'find himself?' They push off many unnecessary responsibilities on us. Don't we need more time just to get to know ourselves?" The other side of that plea for "more time" is your desire for instant adulthood—with all the privileges and freedoms that maturity implies.

Young people are like tender plants. You need healthy conditions (warm concern, nourishment, protection, light and fresh air) and freedom to unfold in your own way. Parents cannot *make* their young grow up at a given rate of speed. They can only provide the conditions for a teenager to progress into an independent, responsible, and productive citizen.

It's hard for parents to let go their children's hands and see them walking independently away. Your mother scolds regressive behavior, like an unkempt room or tardy lessons. Your dad tends to keep everything as smooth, cozy, and comfortable as possible—to put a protective face of stability on social upheaval, hurts, and changes. Sooner or later, the masks come down and you discover the not-so-quiet desperation your parents face as you sail through school. It's tough for them, too.

Your dad gets transferred. If he keeps his job with the company where he's built ten years of seniority, you must move to Chicago or Tulsa or Charlotte. Schools are different, people are different, and you bitterly blame your father for moving. Remember, when you feel at your uncooperative worst, he didn't choose to move. He had to or start over with a new firm.

Some parents try to run their kids' risks for them. To quote a Rye, New York, father with teenage sons in two different colleges: "Any curious youngster at some point in high school or college is going to experiment a little—they always have. But what's lying around for grabs today is a little scary; wide-open sex, right on the campus, all kinds of drugs, Communist front groups that could blackmail you for life. My parents had to worry whether I'd get suspended for breaking curfew. I have to worry whether my sons will disappear into some strange off-beat life before they ever know what they're leaving behind." See? Your risks are tougher.

By "growing up free' I imply *free* of neurotic hang-ups, of anxieties that can cripple you for life, not libertinism (immorality). Of course, your values are fluid, adaptable, and different from your parents' ideals. Yet, you need to be discriminating, selecting wisely from past and present beliefs, while forging a meaningful future.

So that you may test your growth against definite criteria of maturity, here are some characteristics which psychiatrists call "ideal."[31] How would you respond to these questions?

—Am I relatively free of parasitic dependence upon my parents?

—Can I relate to my parents constructively for their growth?

—Is faith more a matter of caring relationships than keeping rules?

—Can I risk myself in social relationships with others so that they sense I care for them, not just myself alone?

—Do I accept my maleness or femaleness and live with mature sexual attitudes toward men and women?

—Have I learned to discipline aggression (anger, hate, cruelty, revenge) so that my relationships are creative, not destructive? The mature adult is parental (loving) and creative, not infantile (demanding or destructive).

—Do I possess a firm sense of reality, relatively free of distortions in outlook and prejudices against persons who are different from myself?

—Am I future-oriented—trusting God, myself, others, and history—able to believe the best and optimistically to work for human betterment? Or am I anxious, mistrusting, guilty over childish impulses, and hung-up in the past?

—Can I enjoy both celebrative play and responsible activities and keep them in proper balance?

If your answer is yes to most of these standards of maturity and good mental health, you are growing. Again, these are ideals. Few adults achieve full maturity. Most of us function in spite of blind spots, anxieties, and unhealthy defenses. We learn to accept ourselves and grow when possible.

"What about religious hang-ups like living on a treadmill?" you ask. In *How to Be a Christian Without Being Religious* Fritz Ridenour exposes games like "playing church" and "purchasing fire insurance." He suggests that religious freedom comes, not in empty rules and rituals, but in response to God's gift in Christ.

Born to Move

Right now, you may not feel like you're taking hold of life. Though born to move ahead, pressures and problems may be pushing you backward. "I just can't concentrate except thinking about problems, daydreaming, and things of this nature," said a high-school senior. His alcoholic mother had been institutionalized. Al suffered daily little dyings.

"How can I keep the growing edge (my healthy self) growing?" you wonder. A psychiatrist, Robert Glen, has said: "There is always something growing in human beings with which you can make an alliance." Think about it, for it's true.

Here is my own philosophy of growth to strengthen your move toward maturity. Even though you don't always do the things you feel you should, and you've failed before, I shall assume the best about you. I believe you desire maturity and will help life to happen for yourself and others around you. If so:

Keep growing from mistrust to faith. Admit it. We are half-open people, suspicious of others, peering through the chinks in our armor. Someone's faith in me helps me find faith in myself. Another's love inspires my self-confidence. Once open to others, I risk myself—become vulnerable—like saying, "Hi, how are things going?" *first* for a change.

Keep growing from absence to being "there" with others. Martin Buber, the late Jewish philosopher, called this moving from "I-it" to human "I-thou" relationships. When we're all wrapped up in our small, snug cocoons there's no room for people in our world. Life offers us daily chances to be present, not absent, with others: parents, teachers, friends.

Keep growing from phoniness to the courage of your own imperfections. Nobody's perfect! People who wear masks, self-concealing phonies, fear honest self-revelation. Needing approval, fearing loss of face, they play the hypocrite game. If you dislike phoniness, you would agree with Jesus Christ who said to some men one day: Outwardly you look fine, but there's rotten stuff inside you (Matt. 23:28, free translation).

Keep growing from despair to discovery. Maybe you are sort of free, yet mostly stymied, in your situation. Your friends grow *up* while you just grow *older*. You want to change.

The common denominator in religious conversion and effective psychotherapy is *desire for change.* You will grow from the inside, not just taller, when you discover new growth patterns. If, for example, you need more privacy, go after it; don't just complain about the noise—try the library or tune out the radio. Encourage pushy parents to provide a private room.

Keep growing from holding grudges to forgiveness. Hans Selye wrote in *The Stress of Life* that revenge kills more people than any other strong emotion. Some teenagers are mad, hurt at what life has done to them. Others suffer guilt and remorse because of what they have done to life. In any case, it is costly to continue as a poor loser, with an ugly self-image, with destructive desires. New resolves like, "Honest, Mom, I'll clean up my room every day," tend to fade. But practicing *and* receiving forgiveness, human and divine, is the turnpike toward maturity.

Keep growing from smugness to humble gratitude. It's easy for a teacher to think he has "the word"; for a parent to feel that his word is "the law"; and a law enforcement officer to "play God." Both smug scientists and pompous ministers are tempted to think they "have it made." And an egotistical teen-ager can give all adults a hard time. You won't have to write a book on "My Humility and How I Achieved It" to develop gratitude. Just thank the powers that be for your great chance at life. Then don't "blow it"; be kind. Others also suffer.

Keep growing from anxiety to decisions for action. You get a lot of data from your technological environment. The *soundaroundus* is deafening! TV, movies newspapers, the *Playboy* philosophy, space ventures, politics, rumors, and extremist's tactics. It's asking a lot to expect you to decode the information, then discard the "hogwash," all at age sixteen.

"What if I fail?" you ask. "There are so many decisions to make right now." Mercifully, God calls for personal integrity but he knows perfection on earth will not be achieved. He expects his people to live faithfully with the light they have. His help, what the Bible calls grace, sees us through. So, take hope, for here and hereafter.

Christian hope suggests that we are destined for a city, beyond the cities of man. It is not just any place. The New Testament book of Revelation suggests that it is a city of perfection, without pain, where there is no more crying. With God in charge, it shall be a life of eternal light, victorious power, and true joy. History points to a cosmic victory which, by faith, you can share. Yes you can!

Psychiatrist Richard Huelsenbeck moved back to his native Switzerland after living thirty-four years in New York City. In an article: "Reflections on Leaving America for Good" he answered his own question—Why? It was not disappointment.

Rather, "I left America because I felt I would never succeed in becoming an American in my heart." It's tough growing up. Hopefully, you will succeed in becoming a real person at heart. That is my earnest wish for you. All the best as you try!

Notes

[1]Erik H. Erikson, *Identity and the Life Cycle* (New York: International Universities Press, 1959), pp. 122-32.

[2]Cited in Preface by Edward B. Lindaman, *Thinking in the Future Tense* (Nashville: Broadman Press, 1978).

[3]Joseph B. Mow, "Jean-Paul Sartre: Christian Theist?" *The Christian Century* (Nov. 23, 1966), 1437-39.

[4]Haim G. Ginott, *Between Parent and Teenager* (New York: The Macmillan Co., 1969), p. 30.

[5]"The Survival of Dana," CBS-TV, May 29, 1979.

[6]From the *New American Standard Bible.* Copyright © The Lockman Foundation, 1960, 1962, 1963, 1971, 1972, 1973, 1975. Used by permission. Subsequent quotations are marked NASB.

[7]From *The Good News Bible,* the Bible in Today's English Version. Old Testament: Copyright © American Bible Society, 1976. New Testament: Copyright © American Bible Society, 1966, 1971, 1976. Used by permission. Subsequent quotations are marked TEV.

[8]Erik H. Erikson, *Identity and the Life Cycle* (New York: International Universities Press, 1959), pp. 88-94.

[9]Abraham H. Maslow, *Toward a Psychology of Being,* 2d ed. (Princeton: D. Van Nostrand Co., Inc., 1968), p. 60.

[10]Charles Wibbelsman, M.D. and Kathy McCoy, *The Teenage Body Book* (New York: Pocket Books, 1979).

[11]Florence Levinsohn and Lombard Kelly, M.D., *A Doctor Discusses What Teenagers Want to Know* (Chicago: Budlong Press, 1961 and 1975. Cf.) *A Doctor's Sex Guide for Patients,* Ibid.

[12]Merton P. Strommen, *Five Cries of Youth* (New York: Harper & Row, 1974), pp. 12-51.

[13]C. W. Brister, *Take Care* (Nashville: Broadman Press, 1978), pp. 81-96.

[14]"Twin girls born to 10-year-old," *Fort Worth Star-Telegram,* June 1, 1979, page 1; "Woman 'pregnant' 70 years," Ibid., June 2, 1979, page 2a.

[15]Office of Adolescent Pregnancy Programs. U.S. Dept. of Health, Education, and Welfare, *Parade,* June 10, 1979., p. 7.

[16]Cited in Charlie W. Shedd, *The Stork Is Dead* (Waco: Word Books, 1968), pp. 61-63.

[17]Evelyn M. Duvall, *Why Wait Till Marriage?* (New York: Association Press, 1965), pp. 112-15.

[18]Lindaman, *Thinking in the Future Tense,* p. 158.

[19]William H. Grier and Price M. Cobbs, *Black Rage* (New York: Basic Books, 1968; Bantam ed., 1969), pp. 112-13.

[20]See Sidney B. Simon, Leland W. Howe, and Howard Kirschenbaum, *Values Clarification* (New York: Hart Publishing Co., 1972).

[21]The author is indebted to a team of psychiatrists and social workers who reported findings of a National Institute of Mental Health study, "Coping Strategies in a New Learning Environment," in Kaoru Yamamoto (ed.), *The College Student and His Culture: An Analysis* (Boston: Houghton Mifflin Co., 1968), pp. 331-44.

[22]Ernst Mayr, *Animal Species and Evolution* (Cambridge, Mass.: Harvard University Press, 1963).

[23]In addition to assistance from your school guidance counselor, practical methods for assessing what you want to accomplish in life appear in Arthur F. Miller and Ralph T. Mattson, *The Truth About You* (Old Tappan, N.J.: Fleming H. Revell Co., 1977).

[24]See, for example, Harry Browne, *You Can Profit from a Monetary Crisis*, Rev. ed. (New York: Macmillan Publishing Co., 1974; Bantam Books, 1975).

[25]Jack Mitchell, "Teen Pregnancy—How to Cope," *Parade*, June 10, 1979, p. 4.

[26]"Sinfully Together," *Time*, July 9, 1979, p. 55.

[27]*Marijuana and Health*. Fifth Annual Report to the U.S. Congress from the Secretary of Health, Education, and Welfare, 1975. Washington, D.C.: United States Government Printing Office.

[28]See Lorene H. Stone, Alfred C. Miranne, and Godfrey J. Ellis, "Parent-Peer Influence as a Predictor of Marijuana Use," *Adolescence*, Spring, 1979, pp. 115-22.

[29]*Fort Worth Star-Telegram*, January 4, 1970, p. 16-A.

[30]Stanley Yolles, M.D., with Charles and Bonnie Remsberg, "An Expert Answers Teen-Agers' Questions About Drugs," *Family Weekly*, March 8, 1970, pp. 4-5.

[31]Leon J. Saul, *Emotional Maturity: The Development and Dynamics of Personality* (Philadelphia: J. B. Lippincott Co., 2d ed., 1960), pp. 3-24. Also see, James Dobson, *Preparing for Adolescence* (Santa Ana, CA.: Vision House Publishers, 1978).